About Island Press

Since 1984, the nonprofit organization Island Press has been stimulating, shaping, and communicating ideas that are essential for solving environmental problems worldwide. With more than 1,000 titles in print and some 30 new releases each year, we are the nation's leading publisher on environmental issues. We identify innovative thinkers and emerging trends in the environmental field. We work with world-renowned experts and authors to develop cross-disciplinary solutions to environmental challenges.

Island Press designs and executes educational campaigns, in conjunction with our authors, to communicate their critical messages in print, in person, and online using the latest technologies, innovative programs, and the media. Our goal is to reach targeted audiences—scientists, policy makers, environmental advocates, urban planners, the media, and concerned citizens—with information that can be used to create the framework for long-term ecological health and human well-being.

Island Press gratefully acknowledges major support from The Bobolink Foundation, Caldera Foundation, The Curtis and Edith Munson Foundation, The Forrest C. and Frances H. Lattner Foundation, The JPB Foundation, The Kresge Foundation, The Summit Charitable Foundation, Inc., and many other generous organizations and individuals.

The opinions expressed in this book are those of the author(s) and do not necessarily reflect the views of our supporters.

My Kind of City

My Kind of City
Collected Essays of Hank Dittmar

Hank Dittmar

Washington | Covelo | London

Copyright © 2019, Henry Eric Dittmar

All rights reserved under International and Pan-American Copyright Conventions. No part of this book may be reproduced in any form or by any means without permission in writing from the publisher: Island Press, 2000 M Street, NW, Suite 650, Washington, DC 20036

ISLAND PRESS is a trademark of the Center for Resource Economics.

Library of Congress Control Number: 2019932650

All Island Press books are printed on environmentally responsible materials.

Manufactured in the United States of America
10 9 8 7 6 5 4 3 2 1

Keywords: Architecture, Athena Award, climate adaptation, Congress for the New Urbanism (CNU), Lean Urbanism, London, The Prince's Foundation for Building Community, rail transport, Reconnecting America, Surface Transportation Policy Project (STPP), sustainable design and planning, transit-oriented development

Contents

Note from the Publisher xiii
Foreword by Andrés Duany xv
Preface by Lynn Richards xix

Part 1. My Kind of Town 1

New Orleans Is My Kind of Town, *Architecture Today* 3
Auckland: At Water's Edge 6
I Could Learn to Love LA All Over Again, Planetizen 8
My Favorite Street: Seven Dials, Covent Garden, London, England
 From *Street Design: The Secret to Great Cities and Towns* by
 John Massengale and Victor Dover 10

Part 2. The Cavaliers vs. the Roundheads 13

Style Wars Are Irrelevant when Architecture Is Reduced to
 Floor-Plate Cladding, Building Design 15
Southbank Scheme Isn't Wrong, It's Just Bland, Building Design 18
When Will Stirling Laureates Be Allowed to Quote from Wren?,
 Building Design 20
People in Glass Houses, Building Design 22
Continuity or Contrast: Take Your Pick, Building Design 24
Three Classicists: Classicism in an Era of Pluralism, From *Three
 Classicists: Drawings and Essays,* by Ben Pentreath, George
 Saumarez Smith, and Francis Terry 26

Part 3. Continuity and Context 29

Continuity and Context in Urbanism and Architecture: The Honesty of a Living Tradition, *Conservation Bulletin* 59 31

Linking Lincoln: Legacy, Ecology and Commerce, from "Pienza: Legacy, Continuity and Tradition," Seaside Pienza Institute 35

Part 4. Bouquets and Brickbats 41

London's Skyscraper Designers Should Aim High Like Chicago, Building Design 43

An Urbanist's View of the Stirling Shortlist, Building Design 45

Don't Students Need Proper Housing?, Building Design 48

The Urbanist's Stirling Prize, Building Design 50

Location Dictates the Success of Monument Design, Building Design 52

It's Time for a New Serpentine Design Brief, Building Design 54

Part 5. Sustainability and Tradition 57

Sustainability and Tradition 59

Part 6. On Christopher Alexander's Athena Award 75

Part 7. Urbanism in Late-Stage Capitalism 81

Post-Truth Architecture in the Age of Trump, Building Design 83

Finally, Some Smart Thinking About Garden Cities, Building Design 85

Garden Towns Need Some Garden City Thinking to Succeed, Building Design 88

Here's the Detail That's Missing from All the Manifestos, Building Design 91

Letter to Edward Glaeser in Response to "Two Green Visions: the Prince and the Mayor," in *Triumph of the City* 94

Can Smart Urban Design Tackle the Rise of Nationalism? Building Design 98

2011 Founders Forum on the New Urbanism at Seaside, Florida, Contribution to an Unpublished Book 101

Architects are Critical to Adapting our Cities to Climate Change, Building Design 112

You've Got to Hand it to Post-Modernism, Building Design 115

Part 8. Lean Urbanism: Making Small Possible 119

A Lean Urbanism for England: Making Small Possible and Localism Real, LeanUrbanism.org 121

Pink Zones To Lighten Planning Red Tape, Building Design 129

Big Ideas Don't Often Produce Great Architecture, Building Design 132

Riding the Railroad to Revival, Building Design 134

Urban Recycling and Doubling-Up: How Cities Really Respond to Growth, Building Design 137

How to Diversify Housing Delivery With Some Help from Architects, Building Design 140

Seeing Empty Homes as an Asset, Not a Liability, Building Design 143

Part 9. About London 147

London's Tall Buildings Bloopers, Building Design 149

A Towering Mess that the Government has the Power—But not the Will—to Address, Building Design 152

Just Because the Powell & Moya Site Is Available Doesn't Mean It's the Right Place for a Concert Hall, Building Design 155

Old Street Will Need More Than Money, Building Design 157

We Need Real Homes, not Ivory Towers, Building Design 159

Bigging up Battersea: A Progress Report, Building Design 161

Are We Serious About Estate Regeneration?, Building Design 163

London's Housing Problems are Beyond the Power of Market Forces to Solve, Building Design 166

Part 10. From Place to Place 169

A Greener, More Pleasant Vision for Travel and Transport, *The Ecologist* 171

Why We Can't Afford to Miss the Train, Building Design 177

Beauty Isn't a Dirty Word, Building Design 179

Highway Capital and Economic Productivity, Reconnecting America 181

Testimony before US Senate Commerce Committee in Air and Rail, 2003, US Senate Committee on Commerce, Science, & Transportation, Amtrak 185

Sprawl: The Automobile and Affording the American Dream, From *Sustainable Planet*, by Juliet Schor and Betsy Taylor 196

Why We Need to Get Beyond the Automated Highway System, Presentation to the National Automated Highway System Assessment Committee, National Academy of Sciences 213

Thinking Like a System: Operationalizing Sustainability Through Transportation Technologies, ITS World Congress 218

About the Author 227

Ancient lights, in English property law, the right of a building or house owner to the light received from and through his windows. Windows used for light by an owner for 20 years or more could not be obstructed by the erection of an edifice or by any other act by an adjacent landowner. This rule of law originated in England in 1663, based on the theory that a landowner acquired an easement to the light by virtue of his use of the windows for that purpose for the statutory length of time.

—Encyclopedia Britannica

Note from the Publisher

This volume is made up of previously published and new writings by Hank Dittmar that he collected and curated for publication.

We have chosen to set the essays, which range from blog posts to transcriptions of talks, in a consistent format and typeface. We have chosen to correct some obvious and unintentional errors, but have otherwise retained the style and idiosyncrasies of the originals. The British spellings in the essays that were published in the UK have been retained. The American English spellings in the writings previously published in the US have been retained. The new writings have been edited to American English spellings.

Most of the essays first appeared in Hank's column in Building Design (BD). Building Design is the UK's leading online source of news, comment, and reviews keeping architects up to date with the key issues affecting the practice and profession of architecture. BD is the place for architects to go for hard-hitting news and comment and is acknowledged by the profession as the leading forum to debate the issues raised by these stories. Other content includes building studies, book and exhibition reviews, and the WA100 ranking of the world's top architectural practices. BD also runs the highly respected Architect of the Year Awards, which is unique in recognizing a body of work across different sectors. Hank Dittmar was one of BD's longest running columnists, writing his first piece in 2005 and his last just two weeks before his passing in April 2018.

Foreword
Andrés Duany

The value of this collection derives from the personal experience that colors them. The discontinuous episodes of Hank Dittmar's life forced him to address these topics as an outsider and as a generalist. Hank had no choice but to range widely, both professionally and culturally. These essays were written over the course of several careers—in public and nonprofit administration, transportation policy, urban planning, urban design, and community building.

As an example, the pragmatism these essays often display is characteristic of an American—where the term has clearly positive connotations. Yet they are tempered by the Englishman's comfort with the merely reasonable, with which Hank became familiar in his later years.

Hank developed wanderlust growing up as a child of the US Air Force. By the time he graduated from high school, his family had lived in ten cities and three countries. Much of his youth was in California, with year-long stints in Oklahoma, Texas, Wisconsin, Alabama, and France. The three years spent in Seville, Spain taught him to love cities. He then lived in Chicago, Austin, Los Angeles, San Francisco, New Mexico, Washington, DC, and finally settled in London.

At Northwestern University in Chicago, Hank discovered the real American city, admiring the ethnic neighborhoods as well as the tall commercial buildings. There, he was mentored academically by the rhetorician David Zarefsky and the anthropologist Edward T. Hall, and inspired by urban studies Professor John McKnight and the Chicago historian Carl Condit. He was also mentored by the street, volunteering in the Uptown district.

His graduate studies at the School of Architecture in Austin coincided with that forgotten war between hippies and modernists. Despite siding socially with the hippies, he developed an interest in then-modern systems theory—but without losing the ability to absorb useful precedent regardless of whether it was recent or not. Somewhere, well outside academia, he also acquired the notion that urbanism should try to increase the stock of human happiness, and in that way leave the planet a better place.

Hank worked in construction, in outreach to the street gangs of inner-city Chicago, and as a planner for public transport in San Francisco and Santa Monica. He served six years as an airport director, as the manager of a metropolitan government and as the head of a national environmental coalition opposing the highway lobby. Expanding from transport to community design, he served as the CEO of a foundation restoring historic railway stations and building communities around transit. For several of the crucial years, he served as chair of the Congress for the New Urbanism; and for nine years as Chief Executive of Prince Charles's Foundation for Building Community.

All that should account for the extraordinary range of these essays. But collected into one volume, they also reveal an unexpected constancy. It is this: Since his 1980 master's thesis contrasting Le Corbusier's Ville Radieuse and Frank Lloyd Wright's Broadacre City with Christopher Alexander's *A Pattern Language*, he has continued to search for ways to engage place, community and history in order to avoid the tempting formalism of plans.

Another recurring theme is that architecture, urbanism and transport are too important to leave to the experts; that specialists tend to miss the bigger picture; that the endless debate between policies that address social issues and policies that address physical place is futile, as both are needed; and in another synthesis there is the support of both top-down and bottom-up strategies.

Above all, Hank shows a rare sensibility within his profession: He has obviously been much moved by beauty. In these essays, he has contributed to the emerging belief that there are certain aesthetic constants across culture, time and class, and that these can be objectively apprehended and taught.

Grand as that range seems—Hank comes across as exceptionally modest. Over the years I have heard him observe that the grandest among his plans are less successful that the improvisational, small-scale interventions that unlocked the creativity of others. While the unraveling of plans can be disheartening, we have shared in the joy of returning to a place and seeing that they have made a difference—even in the attempt. Such is the tenor of Hank's acquired wisdom.

Preface

"I had to be dragged kicking and screaming to my first
Congress for the New Urbanism....but what I found when I
got [there] altered the course of my life."
—Hank Dittmar, 2011 Founders Forum at Seaside, Florida

The Hank Dittmar who said this is the Hank many of us remember: bracing, sometimes blunt, yet open-minded and passionately committed to doing good. These were the qualities that made him such a stunning leader in community planning and design for more than twenty years. Hank's career was marked by achievements in many fields—transportation, land use planning, urban design—and on many levels of practice, from municipal management to federal policy, from grassroots engagement and advocacy to technical assistance and analysis. Hank was also, as evidenced by the essays in this volume, a thoughtful critic and essayist, equally comfortable commenting on philosophy, politics, street design, civic culture, and architecture. In short, he was a true urbanist, adept at challenging the pre-established lines of practice, in the service of meaningful urban design and community strength.

In the 1990s, just as the Congress for the New Urbanism was being established, Hank became a leader in the movement, among the first transportation professionals to embrace New Urbanism. (Formerly the director of the Santa Monica Airport, Hank then went on to serve as the executive director of the Surface Transportation Policy Project, an upstart coalition that had recently surprised everyone in Washington by breaking open federal transportation funding to create more possibilities for transit, walking, and bicycling.) Hank was an original signer of the Charter for the New Urbanism in 1996, and, in short succession, became an energetic task force member and board member for CNU, assuming the role of board chair from 2003 to 2008. Beginning in 2005, Hank became one of the great champions of city- and town-making on both sides of the Atlantic, as director of the London-based Prince's Foundation from 2005 to 2011, where he achieved the feat of relearning everything he had known as an American urbanist in a British context.

If Hank were here, however, he might say that a highlight of his career was a personal one: the chance to present CNU's first-ever Athena Award for Lifetime Achievement to his inspiration, architect–philosopher Christopher Alexander: "The architect and thinker Christopher Alexander changed my life. His work, along with that of Jane Jacobs and the anthropologists Gregory Bateson and Edward T. Hall, helped me reconcile the dissonance between what I saw and liked in cities and landscape and what I was being taught in school. I have relied on that intellectual framework ever since."

Hank's love of Alexander and other wide-ranging thinkers is typical of how he embraced the many disciplines and philosophies. He had an enormous intellect, yet great humility in the face of new ideas, as well as an instinct for connections among concepts that don't seem related at first glance. His approach to life—and to cities—was to embrace the "messy"—a word he uses to good effect in key passages in this book. As he notes in the opening section (a series of love letters to complicated places), cities are "hard to plan, easy to ruin, yet surprisingly adaptable and resilient."

Hank's love of plurality and diversity extended to human lives and human traditions. In an article written for *Grist* in 1999 (not included in this volume), he writes about the need for environmentalists to make common cause with small farmers and ranchers to protect New Mexico's water, calling for the need to preserve human traditions alongside natural resources. Similarly, his ultimate respect for the continuity of human knowledge and pragmatic practice caused him to see a path forward for modernists and traditionalists in architecture to unite in the practice of excellence, "beginning again to learn from the past, to look closely at the evidence of everyday life and everyday culture." "Christopher Alexander teaches that at the heart of making place is seeing, and understanding the things that touch us in nature, in our houses and in our cities, and not being afraid to trust our senses, and our emotions. In a hyper rational world, Christopher Alexander has provided an opening to look at questions of quality, of ease of comfort and of beauty, and in aligning these ideas with nature, and with a series of principles in Nature of Order, he has begun to provide us with some tools for thinking about imbedding these qualities in our work."

Some of the essays in this volume are timeless, while some—notably the architectural criticism and essays in the section on transportation—are very much of a time and place. I believe Hank chose to include those essays in order to highlight the historical highlights as well as the enduring conflicts and needs within each of these fields. In the case of transportation, Hank never shied from addressing the gross inequities and failed logic of some of America's federal infrastructure investment decisions—or lack thereof. ("Amtrak was never meant to succeed, and it has fulfilled that expectation," he said before Congress in 2003.) In the case of architecture, Hank steadfastly refused to get bogged down in the debate about traditional and modernist architecture, instead urging that people who care about place should "embrace pluralism" and resist boiling the debate down to a matter of "Cavaliers versus Roundheads."

Hank brought this regard for plurality to his leadership of CNU, noting that "New Urbanism is a movement, not just an organization," and vowing to uphold "the messy vitality of the movement as a core strength, and the role of the CNU not as captain but as the big tent." Hank saw this approach as not only pragmatic but also critically necessary if the task of restoring communities to more walkable, publicly vibrant places is to be realized. Many hands are needed:

> We are engaged in a long-term, multigenerational campaign. And success will involve both perseverance and adaptability. I would argue that we should not be too bound by the structures that have served us in the past. They will be fine. The opportunity exists to imagine some new framings of our collaborative work together, some new platforms from which to project, or to engage in the

repurposing of existing platforms. I think it is time to stir the pot, lest the New Urbanism becoming content with become merely a boutique shop in the suburban mall that is global development.

In the last decade of his life, Hank stirred the pot tirelessly, devoting much of his effort to establishing Lean Urbanism, a movement he cofounded with Andrés Duany of DPZ CoDESIGN and Brian Falk of the Center for Transect Studies. He was an unrelenting advocate for policy, design, and development solutions to reintroduce human-scaled design and development into everyday practice.

Contributing to the end, Hank spent a final few hours in conversation at a favorite pub with longtime friend and transportation expert Sarah Campbell, just weeks before his death, talking with her enthusiastically about efforts underway to restore playgrounds in London. Only a day before he died, Hank posted a substantive listserve comment on edible plantings on urban streets in Britain. "The Incredible Edible Network has grown to over 50 groups, and has a network to help people start up in their community, providing the roadmap, and they have gotten funding to provide technical assistance to new groups," he wrote on April 1. He died peacefully in his sleep two days later. "Full of life to the last day," commented architect and urban planner Steve Coyle.

This book of essays is a joy to read. Hank's writing is smart without being elitist, witty and poetic, succinct and often surprising. I leave you with one sample. "We are a practical set of reformers, composed of practitioners, who must engage in the world as it is, making improvements a bit at a time and building systems and tools that, at the end of the day, have to be grafted onto an existing system" (on Christopher Alexander's Athena Award).

Lynn Richards
President and CEO, Congress for the New Urbanism
November 2018

Part 1.
My Kind of Town

These few pieces are appreciations of cities, written after visits or as commissions. Some cities I have loved deeply over a long period of time, exploring their history and seeking out forgotten places and famous ones. Los Angeles and London certainly fit into that category, and articles remain to be written about northern New Mexico, Chicago, and Austin, Texas.

Other cities I have loved as a visitor, returning again and again, and often seeking out the same favorite places. Of these, New Orleans tops the list for its architecture, its food, its music, and its dysfunction. I didn't expect to fall for Auckland in New Zealand, having long heard it compared unfavorably to Wellington. But Auckland surprised me.

New Orleans Is My Kind of Town

Architecture Today

February 2, 2010

The United States has often been described as a melting pot, but it is really more of a stew, composed of many distinct ingredients with their own flavour blended into a whole. In New Orleans such a stew is called a gumbo, and there are many different kinds of gumbo.

This kind of cultural adaptation in architecture and urbanism can be seen all over the United States, from cities which borrowed English town building traditions like Charleston and Savannah to the modification of the Mediterranean courtyard house to multifamily housing in Southern California. For my money, the most exciting places are those where a variety of cultural and building traditions come together, colliding, mingling and overlaying in ways that create distinct new traditions.

The best American example is New Orleans, renowned as the birthplace of jazz and infamous as the place which was damaged first by Hurricane Katrina and then by the indifference of the government.

New Orleans brings together Spanish, French, English, and American frontier traditions alongside the Indian, Caribbean and African to create a rich mix of influences in food and music, known worldwide.

This "gumbo" can also be found in architecture and urban design. New Orleans was first a French settlement, and the plan of the French Quarter and its riverfront square reflects French ideas about town planning. The architecture of the French Quarter reflects Spanish building codes, interpreted by American and French architects, with thick-walled courtyard buildings, iron balconies and arcades and building to the lot line. The result, after two centuries of use and re-use of these highly adaptable buildings in a hot moist climate, is an amazing patina and an astonishing diversity that somehow retains its charm despite the onslaught of tourists. The same influences can be found in the nearby and less touristy Fauborg Marigny.

Later districts, such as the Garden District, the Irish Channel and the downtown, mix Caribbean building traditions with classical and Victorian influences, modified by the climate and the culture. Local building types, such as townhouses with galleries on the ground and first floor, and centre hall villas with arcades and side yard entrances, draw upon developing craft and gardening traditions.

Vernacular building types such as the room-on-room shotgun and double shotgun house enabled generations of families to attain homeownership at low cost. This owner-built and -occupied housing has in turn enabled the regional art and cuisine to flourish, for the arts works best in a place where one can live cheaply and well. It was not unusual to learn that carpenters were also musicians, in pre-Katrina New Orleans.

The Cuban-American town planner Andres Duany has said that New Orleans is not the least functional American city, as it was often portrayed in the dark days after the 2005 hurricane, but the most functional Caribbean city. In a 2007 article for *Metropolis* magazine, Duany said, "It was possible to sustain the unique culture of New Orleans because housing costs were minimal, liberating people from debt. One did not have to work a great deal to get by."

This has been one of the great challenges after Katrina, and it is a challenge that Brad Pitt's Make It Right houses, all designed to the highest standards by talented architects, were not designed to answer.

These houses—a valuable addition to New Orleans building culture—rely upon substantial donations to make them affordable, and thus address affordability in a different way. By contrast, the Katrina cottages, of which Marianne Cusato's won the People's Choice Design Awards, is the most well-known, could provide attractive, tiny, low-cost manufactured housing.

Clearly another part of the answer must be the revival of a local building tradition, and the training of local craftspeople in both vernacular crafts and in green building.

This is the piece of the challenge that The Prince's Foundation has chosen to address, in partnership with a local trade college and the Preservation Resource Center. We are training young men and women from damaged neighbourhoods in vernacular building, both through a foundation course that teaches drawing, geometry and proportion, and through practical placements that repair damaged houses in the Ninth Ward.

We're finding that the unique culture that is New Orleans is alive and well in these young people, and that their lives are transformed by a programme that reconnects them with the special nature of their city and its architecture. Increasingly it is becoming clear that post Katrina New Orleans will be smaller, different but still a rich and tasty gumbo of a place.

Auckland: At Water's Edge

As a native Californian, I had always heard Auckland and Wellington compared to Los Angeles and San Francisco, respectively. I think the stereotype was mainly about auto dependency. When I visited, I didn't see it. Auckland is an archipelago, much more than Los Angeles, with its vast coastal plain and gridded streets.

The Auckland plan recognizes this essential nature of the city, noting that "urban Auckland is characterized by its outstanding coastal and harbor settings, its narrow isthmus." Coastal settings are emphasized in Auckland through the Waterfront Plan, as are its principles of being public, working, green-blue, connected, and livable. Indeed the spectacularly successful urban design efforts along Auckland's waterfront have been appreciated by the public and the market alike.

The Auckland Plan recognizes that the Auckland metropolitan area is in transition, from the low-density, suburban city surrounding a central business district (CBD) to a more sustainable, twenty-first century model. This model recognizes the active, healthy, and outdoorsy nature of those who live in Auckland, but also their desire for a public life, for lively centers, and for the benefits of urban diversity. So the plan calls for a quality, compact urban form, for walkability and mixed use, and the fruits of this strategy are beginning to be seen with the lane ways, cultural districts, and urban villages popping up around the region, and with a public transport strategy.

I have been struck by the fact that the Auckland Plan's recognition of the region's outstanding coastal setting only finds expression in the Auckland CBD's waterfront, and not in enhancing the region's coastline and waterfront as a whole, as a place to live, work, and play. An astonishing 56 percent of Aucklanders live within one kilometer of the coast, and 97 percent within five kilometers. This stands to reason, when one thinks about the extent of the 3,100 kilometer coastline and its beauty.

This poses a number of challenges, as it helps to scatter the population, increasing driving and making public transport more challenging. Population dispersal along the coast also creates tensions when a working waterfront comes into contact with living and playing. The desire to live near the water becomes harder and harder to satisfy as more land is protected and land values near the coast increase. While statistics are not available specifically for Auckland, New Zealand-wide figures show that people living within one kilometer of the coast are generally both older and wealthier than those living further inland.

Increasing access and housing near the water thus becomes an issue of intensification in certain areas, and the attractiveness of this strategy has already been demonstrated with the successful redevelopment of the Viaduct area into apartments and offices. The Auckland Plan's development strategy does direct more growth along the coastline, but most emphasis seems to be on the Auckland Waterfront, and not on intensification in other key sub-regional centers and waterfront neighborhoods.

As an advocate of TOD, or public Transport-Oriented Development, I am pleased to see that Auckland is developing lively, mixed neighborhoods around its rail system. I think Auckland also needs COD, or Coastal-Oriented Development (not the delicious fish!), that combines mixed-use, multifamily neighborhoods—both apartments and terraces—near selected waterfronts with a gradual strategy of improving waterborne transportation, aka ferry service. Such a strategy could both develop selected new communities at densities that would support ferry service and amenities, such as at Hobsonville Point and Scott Point, and identify coastal brownfield sites near urban centers for infill development of multifamily, mixed neighborhoods.

Concentrating development reduces coastal-zone impact, creates more affordability, and makes ferry service more viable.

Good planning builds upon the advantages a region already has, and what struck me about Auckland was both its beautiful landscape and its intimate relationship with the sea. This is already reflected in the lifestyle of its residents, and planning and development strategies that enhance this identity and character will only increase Auckland's attractiveness and competitiveness globally. That's why I think Auckland needs more COD.

I Could Learn to Love LA All Over Again

Planetizen, 2005

It was fitting that the 13th Congress for the New Urbanism, "Examining the Polycentric City," should be held in Pasadena, California. Southern California, long seen as the epitome of the car-borne culture, has been attempting to remake itself. It reflects how cities all over the world, including London, are confronting new waves of growth, and its effect in both physical and economic terms on the existing city. A number of British urbanists made the trip to Pasadena, continuing the ongoing dialogue between UK urbanists and the American New Urbanists.

Southern California is a land of myths: home of the movie industry, the land of "fruits and nuts," birthplace of surfing, and epicenter of the car culture. These myths have been exported worldwide. Acclaimed theorists from Reyner Banham to Baudrillard have heralded Southern California as the harbinger of a rootless, transitory, anti-historic life, and in the process have contributed to an expectation about cities of the future.

A few of those myths were exploded at the Pasadena event. It emerged that, far from springing up around the car, Southern California was actually built around a network of streetcar routes. The notion that density doesn't exist in the region is equally untrue. The great central plain of Los Angeles has a density-per-mile that is equal to San Francisco, in an area twice the size. Hollywood and Koreatown are as dense as Paris.

However, it was the coming of the freeway which broke up the streetcar grid and led to the biggest Southern California myth of all: that of untrammelled mobility. People were encouraged to believe that the freeways enabled longer commutes at high rates of speed, and more and more traffic was channelled onto a small set of roadways. This hasn't worked, as the iron law of traffic is that building more roads encourages more driving, and more auto-centred development.

Southern California now has a network of commuter rail, light rail and rapid bus routes to network the region, after spending billions of dollars in the process.

British-born New Urbanist Peter Calthorpe presented to the Congress a regional plan for accommodating the region's dramatic growth with high-density nodes of mixed use along public transport corridors.

While the reintroduction of mass transit helps give a skeleton to the new polycentric city, the true heart of Southern California lies in the towns and neighbourhoods that make its many centres. Santa Monica and Pasadena began a trend in reclaiming town centres from in-town malls by reopening streets—clearly a lesson in the way retail may go in future.

Decreasing freeway speeds are forcing busy families to shop and play in their local communities, and those communities are seeking to recapture vitality and active street life.

Most of Southern California is auto-centred sprawl, and most of its residents live in the spaces between the walkable mixed-use centres that are now emerging. That's why reforming national street standards to be context-sensitive, and creating "green" standards for neighbourhood development are so important: they represent fundamental change to the planning and delivery systems for growth.

It's also the CNU's lesson for the UK, struggling with challenges of growth in the Southeast and the problem of uneven development. Southern California's transformation isn't about marketing and re-branding. It marks the rediscovery of the essential qualities of each place by those in the front line: councillors, business groups, environmentalists and immigrants.

My Favorite Street: Seven Dials, Covent Garden, London, England

From *Street Design* by Victor Dover and
John Massengale, 2014

> But what involutions can compare with those of Seven Dials? Where is there such another maze of streets, courts, lanes, and alleys? ... The stranger who finds himself in "The Dials" for the first time, and stands Belzoni-like, at the entrance of seven obscure passages, uncertain which to take, will see enough around him to keep his curiosity and attention awake for no inconsiderable time. From the irregular square into which he has plunged, the streets and courts dart in all directions, until they are lost in the unwholesome vapor which hangs over the house-tops.
> — Charles Dickens, *Sketches*, 1843

My favorite London street is actually the confluence of seven streets near London's Covent Garden into a circular space called the Seven Dials. At the center of the Dials stands an obelisk with six sundials (not seven) donated by the Worshipful Company of Mercers—one of London's guilds, and the owner of the area—in the 1690s.

Designed by Thomas Neale, a speculator who took the area on a lease from the Mercers Company, the area has certainly seen its ups and downs. In Dickens's time, it was part of the infamous St. Giles Rookery, an overcrowded slum famous for violence, prostitution, and brawls between the Irish and the English. With the redevelopment of the Covent Garden Market as an attraction in the 1970s, Seven Dials has grown in popularity, and today is loved by residents and tourists alike.

Over the past two years, the clutter has been removed from nearby streets, granite pavers have been restored in the pavement, and the monument has been cleaned and restored. In traffic-engineering terms, the junction operates as a shared space, with the monument serving as a pedestrian haven and the junction itself used equally by cars, cyclists, and pedestrians. Each of the seven streets is similarly a shared space, and the surrounding area boasts one of London's best coffee roasters; a back court called Neal's Yard with London's best fromagerie; and many delightfully individual cafes and shops, with wares ranging from rare books to secondhand designer clothing. Each street has its own character (one with market stalls), and no matter where one sets out to go, one ends up in an interesting place.

Incidentally, not two blocks away is Central St. Giles— a celebrated new building covering a city block and designed by Renzo Piano—that is the opposite of Seven Dials. The buildings are made of steel and brightly colored glass, and the public space is internal, irrigated neither by cars nor pedestrians. As a result, the retail is struggling—less than a year after Central St. Giles opened to acclaim from some design critics for its contribution to the civic realm.

Comparing the two areas is instructive, for it reveals what makes Seven Dials special. It is part of a densely connected network of small streets, bounded by three- to six-story buildings, with continuous retail, mostly on the small side. While there is a traditional delineation between street and pavement, it is made with paving materials and curbs—and without either the bright colors or railings that have become the default positions of the shared spacers and the engineers, respectively. The monument at the center has an inviting shelf upon which to sit and people-watch; and to get there, pedestrians have to walk across the intersection. Finally, the area is managed for a mix of small unique shops and larger brands, with residential space above and office space nearby.

Traffic engineering is a small but essential part of what makes this a great street. The junction of seven streets could have easily become a no-go area for pedestrians, but the intimate scale of the streets, the quality of the pavement, the calm and understated detailing and materials, and the fine monument at the center of the junction all contribute to make this a space for people where cars are tolerated, and one of my favorite places to be.

Part 2.
The Cavaliers vs. the Roundheads

It sometimes seems that the style wars in architecture have always been with us. To my mind, though, it is John Ruskin whom we really have to blame for the notion that particular styles of architecture are more appropriate, or even more moral, than others. His embrace of the Gothic as Christian and rejection of the Classicist as Pagan leads directly to Pevsner's "spirit of the age" and the notion that traditional architecture is somehow not allowed in the "machine age."

Somehow, though, people kept wanting traditional as well as modernist buildings, and it seems they have always done so. Perhaps it is time to embrace pluralism.

Style Wars Are Irrelevant when Architecture Is Reduced to Floor-Plate Cladding

Building Design

January 14, 2015

The publication of the Prince of Wales's 10 principles of urban design, followed by images of Quinlan and Francis Terry's sketch of a proposal for Hyde Park Barracks and an image of a Robert Adam-designed trio of towers in Reading, has sparked a predictable tut-tutting from outraged critics and architects.

Even those most outraged by Prince Charles's principles, and his temerity to continue having opinions about architecture and urbanism, have had to admit that they agree with many, if not most, of the precepts, however "grudgingly." Few seem to have remarked that in most new projects, these principles—of scale, enclosure, pedestrian orientation and composition—are honoured more with lip service than in actuality.

People are beginning to speculate about a classical revival and bringing out all the old saws about authoritarian regimes and honesty in materials. These epithets seem tired to me when one looks at the ubiquity of contemporary building types and the degree to which they both reflect corporate finance structures and reduce architecture to floor-plate cladding. The antipathy to traditional references seems almost Pavlovian, especially when one considers the degree of consensus about the impact of these trends on the city.

The traditional camp has its own array of catchphrases and well-worn arguments and, as an expat of a decade here, I can still recall being told that the antipathy between modernism and classicism was more vituperative in the UK, reflecting the intensity of the Cavaliers vs the Roundheads.

The debate poorly reflects the actual situation in UK architectural practice, which seems to me to be healthier and more plural and interesting than ever, despite the fact that the bulk of new building, whether residential or office, is still dire. It reminds me, in some ways, of the post-modern era, which to me was far more than simply jokey facades and outsized pediments but rather was about beginning again to learn from the past, to look closely at the evidence of everyday life and everyday culture, and an encouragement of debate after a period when architecture students were force-fed Sigfried Giedion. In addition to the puns, the era gave us the diverse ideas of Christopher Alexander, Leon Krier, Colin Rowe, James Stirling, Aldo Rossi, John Outram and Robert AM Stern.

I see that diversity and pluralism emerging today, in the reconsideration of municipal house building of all eras, in the renewed interest in decoration and ornament, in mid-rise buildings and street-based urbanism, and in a more nuanced approach to building in historic context. Astley Castle and the Everyman Theatre demonstrate that this plurality is recognised by Stirling Prize juries, in what appears to be a turn away from object buildings in space. Significant housing commissions from the Peabody Estates in urban London and Hastoe Housing Group in towns and villages are going to architects that explore truly contextual solutions in a contemporary vein while pushing the envelope in things like passive design and housing typology.

Sometimes I think the style war is generational and that architects just entering their most productive years are not hampered by the blinkers imposed by the battles fought by earlier generations; that they are free to look at and learn from the evidence both on the ground and in the treatises. Classicism is now being taught, not as a dogma, but as a studio practice in a few architecture schools, and this might mean that, like Le Corbusier and Mies van der Rohe, young architects might be able to approach design again with the full resources of their forebears.

All this is indeed encouraging, and it is tempting to try to bury the hatchet. But there is a still larger battle to be fought. The bulk of contemporary building is predetermined by what valuers and developers think the market demands or is prepared to accept. So we find housing in London dictated by the tastes of global investors, with the production of largely identical tall buildings that poorly address the street and little reflect the needs of actual London families or sound people. Architecture is dictated by these floor plates and so whether it is Adam's classically clad towers or projects like the humorously named Canaletto or the zig-zaggy forms of Battersea, the type and the building footprint and impact are largely the same. The same is true of new house-builder housing outside London, with the same house plans and site plans reappearing with traditional, modern or postmodern gob-ons. A whole roster of building, street and landscape typologies are left on the shelf.

Efforts like the Skyline Commission and Create Streets represent the same impulse of architects and others to address this essentially post-modern problem. It is centred in the production process, and the nature of the valuation, marketing and sales processes to repeat the formulas until a market correction happens—then hunker down and repeat again once the dust settles. This is the real problem with architecture and city making, and it is one that the style wars don't address and in fact one in which the style warriors might find a common enemy.

Southbank Scheme Isn't Wrong, It's Just Bland

Building Design

December 20, 2013

Cultural buildings may be the last place where the architect is expected to put art before commerce, and even there the demands of budget and of income generation are growing. Increasingly, cultural buildings are being renewed to meet changing demands.

How architects approach that task, and how they respond to the original vision for the building, is now contested territory.

For many years the cultural convention, enshrined in a narrow interpretation of 1964's Venice Charter, was for the addition to respect the integrity and scale of the original, to be physically separated (usually by glass) and to be of its time. This usually meant different materials and contrasting architectural grammar.

The past half-decade has seen this convention breaking down and a diversity of approaches appearing. These might be lumped into three new categories.

I would call the first type *projects of violation*—and here I would place Daniel Libeskind's Royal Ontario Museum and Zaha Hadid's Serpentine Sackler Gallery, where the architectural language not only contrasts but overpowers by enveloping and subduing the original building.

The second category aims for continuity rather than contrast, and uses the grammar and materials of the original. John Simpson's work at the Queen's Gallery and Kensington Palace comes to mind, along with the Allies & Morrison revamp of the Royal Festival Hall.

In the third category are projects that create a dialogue between old and new, blending materials, techniques and ornament. Witherford Watson Mann's Astley Castle, Chipperfield's Neues Museum and Caruso St John's work at Tate Britain are examples here.

All three approaches reflect a different attitude to history from that of the Venice Charter, which stands as a sort of peace treaty between the modern movement and the emerging conservation profession. History is no longer seen as a series of discrete projects with stops and starts, and neither should architecture be seen this way.

It is useful to frame the Southbank Centre within this dialogue. The area is in the midst of a gold rush, with growth-seeking councils, developers going for the gold, and a competitive hunger to be at the centre of the action.

The centre aims to be the salon for all this activity, and under Jude Kelly's artistic direction it has become a lively mix of cultural venue, food court and nightclub. Kelly has argued persuasively that the complex's architects always intended it to evolve, and against preserving it as a sort of dour monument to brutalism.

I hold no brief for these tired buildings, though I am fond of the Royal Festival Hall, and I am sympathetic to her argument that they can be changed. But the question is whether the Feilden Clegg Bradley scheme measures up, and I agree with most who say the self-styled "glass box" (that isn't one) and the "liner building" neither do justice to the original nor enliven the space. Instead they overpower, becoming a bland project of violation.

The best that can be said about the proposal is that it fits into the emergent SE1 context: developer opportunism using the tropes of the corporate office building and the urban retail venue to maximise floorspace.

When Will Stirling Laureates Be Allowed to Quote from Wren?

Building Design

October 20, 2015

Awarding the Stirling Prize to Allford Hall Monaghan Morris' Burntwood School has been applauded as much for the political statement it makes about investing in good design for schools, as for the architecture. It allowed the profession to recall New Labour's Building Schools for the Future programme at the same time as it honoured a practice which has done a lot of work designing schools.

Equally notable to me was the fact that the architect generously cited his influences, particularly Marcel Breuer, whose work in precast concrete at Boston's Madison Park School clearly inspired the facade of the Burntwood School. Indeed Olly Wainwright argues in The Guardian that it "could have come straight from the drawing board of Marcel Breuer."

Breuer's work spanned decades but his precast concrete buildings were most associated with the Fifties and Sixties and comments about the building have referenced this look back at a creative period in the long historic epoch of modernism.

Perhaps this means it is possible to erase the double standard that seems to exist in architecture, where it is permissible to quote or use modernist precedents, but often forbidden in planning guidance to reference precedents from before the modern era, such as Palladio or Wren or Lutyens. The use of precedent in traditional architecture is derided as "pastiche," a descriptive term which has been transformed into an epithet, or as "historicist," taking history and turning it into a pathology by adding "ist" on the end, as in calling something Islamist rather than Islamic.

A casual look online finds dozens of examples of supplemental planning guidance which instruct applicants to avoid pastiche and to rely on contemporary design. A Bradford document exhorts applicants to "avoid historic styles and pastiche," while the London Borough of Richmond SPG asks designers to "avoid pastiche." The Islington urban design guide says "high-quality contemporary designs will be supported" and "pastiche design that is a poor copy of the original will generally be resisted."

This kind of double standard, where it is celebrated to use the stylistic vocabulary of modernism, including pilotis, podiums, precast and shuttered concrete and so on, but frowned on to employ a base or a capital with a column or a pitched roof is rife within juries, at planning departments and on expert panels.

One wonders when designs which reference Breuer or Mies or the Smithsons will be considered pastiche or historicist rather than contemporary. Buildings built in the Seventies are now receiving the protection of listing and so surely they have passed into history? Surely it is time to put down the cudgel of labelling and look to the quality of the design rather than the precedent employed?

There are signs of change, at least in architectural discourse. The RIBA's Palladio exhibition showcases both classical and contemporary design inspired by Palladio, and manages to show the traditional buildings without snark. The resurgence of interest in post-modernism and work in a post-modernist vein reinforces Charles Jencks's idea that architecture should be plural to reflect an increasingly plural society.

To me this speaks of a richer architecture, one which draws inspiration from the entire treasure trove of the past and abandons the old twentieth-century idea of a single spirit of the age for a design vocabulary that draws from history but allows the architect to add her individual contribution to that ever-growing palette.

Everyone looks at the Stirling Prize for an indication of where architecture is going, and it may be that it is going into opposition to this government. Beyond this political point, this year's Stirling finalists point to a more plural approach to architecture. That said, I won't hold my breath waiting for a Demetri Porphyrios, John Simpson or Craig Hamilton building to be nominated.

People in Glass Houses

Building Design

February 24, 2012

Any issue that brings Ken Shuttleworth and Prince Charles together deserves a second look. Last year, when Ken Shuttleworth said that it was time to stop designing inefficient glass boxes, and that people should accept "a solid wall with a window in," people focused on the press identifying him as the main designer of the Gherkin.

Prince Charles made a similar comment to the Institution of Civil Engineers this month, and it was viewed as another salvo in the style wars, drawing the usual reflexive attack from the RIBA.

Perhaps because the glass wall is such a core precept of modernity for architects, its inherent inefficiency tends to be accepted. So one tries to address glass walls, which leak heat during winter and overheat during summer, by buying another layer of glazing, putting a brise-soleil on the outside of the building, and adding symbolic renewable energy fetishes to the building.

The thermal failure of glass-walled residential towers in Toronto has become a local scandal. Writing in *Building Science*, professor John Straube said, "When I see a fully glazed, floor-to-ceiling commercial or institutional building, I see an energy-consuming nightmare of a building that requires lots of heating and cooling at the perimeter just to maintain comfort." Straube calls for a balance of glazing and wall systems, challenging architects to go past the easy design solution of floor-to-ceiling glass to make beautiful facades.

The 2009 Atelier 10 study commissioned by Robert Adam compared solid-walled buildings with generous punched-out windows to glass-curtain walls, and found a 10–15% reduction in energy costs from the heavier construction. The study also noted significant issues of overheating in office buildings.

Our own Natural House with Kingerlee/NBT at the Building Research Establishment uses solid-walled masonry construction, generous glazing and natural insulation to reach Code 4 without micro-renewables.

Last autumn I revisited Chicago and saw again the early skyscrapers that inspired me as a young man. In the facades of Louis Sullivan, Holabird & Roche and Burnham & Root, I saw an approach that opened up interiors, yet contrasted glass with stone and ceramic and steel, and used proportion and hints of ornament to tell a story far more interesting than that of the oddly shaped glass buildings being generated for corporate clients across the world today. Surely architecture has more to say about the human condition than transparency or mirroring?

The news from Toronto that the entire skin of glass-walled condo towers should be replaced after 15 years must be coupled with the fact that these buildings are seen by many as symbols of the bubble years. Maybe the architecture we need is a long-lived one. This kind of architecture is emerging, in masonry with Hopkins, Cottrell & Vermeulen and Haworth Tompkins, in the use of thermal mass with green designers such as Architype and Justin Bere and in new traditional work. Perhaps as energy prices rise and life-cycle costs bite, commissioners will begin to respond.

Continuity or Contrast: Take Your Pick

Building Design

November 30, 2012

I have just returned from Beijing, where I had the chance to reflect on issues of change and context in architecture, what responsibilities an architect has to the collective memory of a place, and how best to reflect history in new and old buildings. Context and memory loom large in China, both because of the tremendous upheaval of the Cultural Revolution and because of the huge change wrought by its emergence as a global economic superpower.

I want to discuss three projects: Zaha Hadid's Galaxy Soho project, opened last month to a crowd of Beijing socialites and design illuminati; the careful restoration of a "hutong" courtyard as a hotel; and an older project to reframe Beijing's single-family courtyards as multi-family, higher-density living space. Each represents a different approach to the problem of context.

Hadid's Galaxy Soho is a striking, curvy object alongside a motorway. A real ground-scraper, it is organised around a flowing series of internal spaces, described by the PR flackery as being inspired by the courtyard housing that it replaced. To me it resembled a wavy version of a big shopping mall. Indeed, instead of semi-private spaces for family life, Galaxy Soho presents privatised spaces for conspicuous consumption and office work. Its approach to context is one of contrast, with a lashing of appropriation.

Courtyard Seven reuses a courtyard in the Dongcheng district as a hotel. Immaculately restored using recycled materials and traditional skills, with contemporary amenities and geothermal heating, the project sits within a functioning hutong neighbourhood, just down the street from a lively food market. It introduces new life into the hutong, and re-imagines a future for the single-storey courtyard as accommodation for visitors and perhaps creative industries—a new context but one of continuity and adaptation rather than difference.

The Ju-er Courtyard Housing Project, by Tsinghua University professor Wu Liangyong, won a UN Habitat award in 1993. It sought to create a new residential courtyard typology that would be multi-storey and multi-family. Providing internal spaces within the building perimeter, the architecture seemed to borrow more from the suburban garden apartment type than from the courtyard apartment or mansion block. Beijing people told me it had not been that popular, and perhaps this was due to compromises made in the building process. It certainly suffered by comparison to the courtyards around it.

Nonetheless, its approach was a worthy one: attempting to learn from heritage and evolve it to meet present-day needs—clearly the old model of a single courtyard for a single family is not viable in Beijing today. I am planning to explore further the idea of preserving a series of internal chambers for family life, protected from the busy street, and evolving the type for multi-family living.

The emergence of a range of different approaches to context, ranging from patch and repair to adaptation and evolution, begins to add nuance to the fundamentalist approach to conservation found in the Venice Charter of the 1960s. It's all heritage, after all.

Three Classicists: Classicism in an Era of Pluralism

Originally published in Three Classicists: Drawings and Essays *by Ben Pentreath, George Saumarez Smith, Francis Terry, The Bardwell Press, 2010*

For the average British family, their home is not only their castle, it is their largest investment, and their pension. Small wonder that, according to the Environmental Change Institute's Brenda Boardman, "the present rate of demolition in the UK is low—resulting in less than 0.01 percent of the stock being demolished each year and implying that the stock is replaced once every 1,300 years."

Of course, when this is applied to the new flats delivered over the past decade or so, this is absurd, as they will be lucky to last 50 years. However, for the millions of owner-occupied prewar houses in Britain there is a positive disincentive to demolition, and so long as the house is a family's biggest investment we ought to consider building for hundreds of years, rather than for a few decades.

It is useful to think of sustainability—by now a word almost leached of meaning—in its original definition of having the capability of being sustained, otherwise long-lived. Long-lived buildings tend not to be too trendy or fashionable, tend to be solid, made of masonry, and tend to be well loved, hence cared for over time. We are increasingly finding out that these kind of classical, solid-walled, thermally efficient masonry buildings can exhibit superior environmental performance.

I would bet on the work of these three classicists—elegant but not trendy, solidly crafted, and careful—as being as well or better loved in a hundred or two hundred years as it is today. Much of their work is in the domestic realm, whether in country and town houses or production building, and this reflects the preference of many British people for traditional architecture.

Ben Pentreath, George Saumarez Smith and Francis Terry can draw as well as they design, and their drawings demonstrate their command of proportion, of detail and of the line. The RIBA has always rightly celebrated drawing by architects, and its collection of drawings in the Victoria and Albert Museum is unparalleled.

The drawings in this catalog demonstrate that architectural drawing is still relevant, even in the era of AutoCAD and Sketchup, and that hand drawing can persuade, beguile and teach in a way that the precision of the computer never will.

In its urban design and building crafts courses, The Prince's Foundation still stresses drawing by hand, not in opposition to the use of the computer, but as essential to training the eye to see and the hand to reveal what is seen. This link between drawing and design skill is revealed in the beautiful details of Francis Terry, in the innovative country houses drawn by George Saumarez Smith and in the simple and refined terraces of Ben Pentreath. It is instructive that all three received an unconventional architectural education, and learned to draw by working alongside traditional architects rather than through architecture schools.

Each of the three designers has contributed three short essays, which together make some important points about their work. Taken together, they lead me to two conclusions. First, they speak to me of craft and materiality, rather than of avant-garde art and metaphor. Theirs is an approach to architecture that is immediately practical, however rooted in beauty and skill. The comparison between buildings and food is a particularly telling one, grounding the making of buildings among the basic human needs rather than in the abstraction of textual analysis.

Finally, all three men exhibit a refreshing lack of worry about the great style debate that has so enfeebled British architecture over the past fifty years. Francis Terry, George Saumarez Smith and Ben Pentreath are confident classicists, happy to work in a plural world. They are free of the compulsion to be jokey or ironic about decoration or the use of the orders that characterised so much of the classical revival that followed postmodernism, and they are free of the opposite tendency to stripped neoclassicism that followed the introduction of modernism. As they and their peers across the architectural spectrum respond to a post-carbon, post-fossil fuel, post-speculation era, it will be interesting to see their architecture evolve. I rather suspect that it will reveal that classicism is a living language in the hands of an engaged new generation.

Part 3. Continuity and Context

Morris and Ruskin reacted to the Victorian trend for rebuilding churches by arguing that one should patch rather than rebuild heritage. Over time this has led to a heritage ideology that new alterations or additions to historic buildings should be visually different from the original structure.

Like much architectural theory, this is descended from the Twentieth Century notion of history as a series of projects—the Enlightenment Project, the Modern Project, and so on. While useful in this classroom, this idea elides the fact that history is continuous that ideas as well as buildings express the diversity of humankind, not a consensus.

Part 3: Continuity and Context

Continuity and Context in Urbanism and Architecture: The Honesty of a Living Tradition

Conservation Bulletin

Issue 59: Autumn 2008

Reproduced with permission of Historic England, HistoricEngland.org.uk

As an American who moved to Britain to take up post at the Prince's Foundation, I anticipated a collegial partnership between conservation architects and those concerned with historic fabric and people like myself planning new development that was sensitive to the environment and human scaled. Certainly, as an urbanist concerned about the negative impacts of 20th-century sprawl and the other detritus of modern-movement theories of the city, I had always enjoyed a robust partnership with what is called the preservation community in the US.

I was therefore surprised when perfectly charming senior figures in the UK heritage sector assured me that there was little commonality between the discipline of the conservation profession and what they saw as the ersatz world of Poundbury, an attitude discordant with our President's view that a living tradition could unify the architecture of the past with that of the present.

Over the past two years, in our own projects and in a series of discussions with the National Trust Architectural Panel. The Prince's Foundation has evolved a series of principles for building in an historic context. These principles were launched by HRH The Prince of Wales at a conference on New Buildings in Old Places. There are five core ideas.

- Recognition that sustainability means building for the long term—one hundred years, rather than twenty years.
- Because of this, building in an adaptable and flexible manner, reassessing and reusing existing buildings wherever possible.
- Building in a manner that fits the place, in terms of materials used, proportion and layouts and climate, ecology and building practices.
- Building beautifully, in a manner that builds upon tradition, evolving it in response to present challenges and utilising present-day resources and techniques.
- And finally, understanding the purpose of a building or group of buildings within the hierarchy of the buildings around it and responding with an appropriate building type and design. Doing this often implies composition of a harmonious whole, rather than the erection of singular objects of architectural or corporate will.

We think that these principles should apply whether building anew or adapting existing buildings, as sustainability is achieved by creating buildings that people will both want to use, and be able to use efficiently, a hundred years hence. I think that most Britons would agree that local distinctiveness should flourish and traditional craft skills be re-discovered and incorporated in new buildings as well as old; that true and timeless methods of building are exploited not only for the beauty they create, but also for the environmental benefits they offer.

Planners working in and near conservation and heritage areas can do far worse than ensure that new development works with rather than against the pattern of existing streets, blocks and plots, and architects should revisit traditional typologies and the vernacular, adapting and evolving them in response to present needs. I was intrigued to read how Newham Council recently declared a quite ordinary collection of old industrial buildings in Sugar House Lane, Stratford, as a Conservation Area with the express purpose of managing change—in the very shadow of the Olympic site—for better place-making.

The Prince's Foundation believes in learning through practice, and so we undertake live urban design and master-planning projects to develop new tools and deliver exemplar solutions to Britain's core development problems. By way of example, in 2005, we were asked to undertake an Enquiry by Design leading to a new Area Action Plan for the 2000-year-old city centre of Lincoln. Following the successful completion of that effort, we have remained involved to help guide urban regeneration in Lincoln, and have held two summer schools in architecture and building crafts on the grounds of Lincoln Cathedral.

Lincoln's core reason for being was its location at the crossing of the river at Brayford Pool, and its place athwart the great Roman route north—the Fosse Way—and Ermine Street. It draws its character from the relationship between the river and the hill. The Roman fort on the hill translated into the castle, marketplace and cathedral with high street below, giving shape to a remarkably stable street network based on the relationship between culture, government and commerce, which can be traced through almost two thousand years of Lincoln's history. The river and the Brayford Pool, which brought people to the place originally, continued to define the shape of the city's street pattern for almost as long.

In his book *How Buildings Learn: What Happens After They Are Built*, American author Stewart Brand introduced the concept of pace layering, meaning that different parts of a building—or a city—change at different rates. When applied to civilisation, pace layering implies that certain deep structures, like the relationship between a city and nature, or the culture of a city, ought to change slowly, while other activities, like entertainment or retail, shift more quickly, and need to be accommodated in a flexible manner within these more permanent layers of the city. I have used Brand's basic notion as a template for a legacy-based plan for Lincoln.

When we looked at Lincoln during our workshops, we found that the city centre had been altered dramatically in the past century and half for the sake of more transitory functions, such as retail trends or commercial speculation. Transport interventions, including an at-grade railway and elevated roadways, have cut off circulation between the city centre and supporting neighbourhoods. Recent building developments have further altered the basic structure of streets and pedestrian movement, walling off the river, hampering movement across the city and destroying continuity with a rich building tradition. As all of these interventions approach the end of their useful life, we have through our Enquiry by Design methodology identified opportunities to create an enduring framework for the town centre that enables it to adapt flexibly to change while respecting the legacy of this ancient city, and to restore its basic circulatory system.

At the scale of the individual building, the Foundation shares cause with conservation professionals in looking to both maintain and enhance traditional building skills not just for heritage settings, but also in order to apply them as a core part of our 'eco-vernacular' approach to architecture. Clearly, natural materials do not require the high levels of industrial processing that have given us today's palette of UPVC windows, plastic membranes, and their like. We have moved from the regular use of 500 building materials in 1919 to 500,000 today! Most of these have high-energy loads in their production, and their long-term implications are unknown. In a project partnering with the Building Research Establishment, we are demonstrating that a traditionally built home with solid-wall construction can meet modern energy-performance standards, and will make an attractive proposition for the average homebuyer. At the same time we are promoting the retention of heritage stock that can be upgraded to higher energy-efficiency standards. The value of continuing and developing skills in lime-based mortars and cements, clay, cob and thatch, traditional working of wood and stone, is recognised in this context as being as important as the application of photovoltaics, wind turbines and the like. Craft skills are thus part of the Green debate.

The Venice Charter, adopted early in the Cold War period, has been interpreted to mean that we ought to express difference rather than continuity when building in the historic environment. After two or three cycles of experimentation with unproven theories of urban planning and design, perhaps it is time that we reconsider the outmoded ideas of the early 1960s, and look for an approach that stresses continuity and evolution, accepting the best of the past and evolving tradition to take on contemporary challenges.

Linking Lincoln: Legacy, Ecology and Commerce

From *Pienza: Legacy, Continuity and Tradition*, Seaside Pienza Institute, 2007

"Fashion changes quickly, Commerce less quickly, Infrastructure slower than that, then Governance, then Culture, and slowest is Nature. The fast parts learn, propose, and absorb shocks; the slow parts remember, integrate, and constrain. The fast parts get all the attention. The slow parts have all the power."
—Stewart Brand

"A bicycle shed is a building, Lincoln Cathedral is a piece of architecture."
—Nikolaus Pevsner

In 2005, The Prince's Foundation was asked to undertake an Enquiry by Design leading to a new long range plan for the city centre of Lincoln, a two-thousand-year-old city in the English midlands. Following the successful completion of that effort, the Foundation remained involved to help guide urban extensions in Lincoln, and has held a summer school in architecture and building crafts on the grounds of the Lincoln Cathedral. (At the five-year mark, the City reaffirmed its commitment to the master plan framework agreed upon with The Prince's Foundation.)

Lincoln is an ancient city, with ancient strengths and virtues. Its core reason for being has resided in its location at the crossing of the river at Brayford Pool, and its place athwart the great Roman route north—the Fosse Way—and Ermine Street. It further draws its character, and that of its citizens, from the relationship between the river and the hill. Over the centuries, this relationship between Lincoln and its place in nature has helped to shape a series of remarkably enduring parts of the city, which in turn create enduring relationships with the generations inhabiting and visiting Lincoln.

The Roman fort on the hill and the marketplace became the castle and the cathedral on the hill and the high street below, giving shape both to a remarkably stable street network and to a relationship between culture, government and commerce that can be traced through almost two thousand years of Lincoln's history. And the river and the Brayford Pool, which brought people to the place originally, continued to define the shape of the city's street pattern for almost as long, until the intervention of the Victorian railway and the post-war high-speed road networks severed the city centre from the neighbourhoods which depend upon it and upon which it depends.

Indeed, when participants in The Prince's Foundation's workshops at Lincoln were asked to identify the essential qualities of the city, these enduring relationships emerged as foremost: the relationship between the city and the Cathedral; the walkability of the city centre; the friendliness of the city and its inhabitants; the scale of the place; and the fact that Lincoln is an old city which still functions and adapts well to change. Most of these points may be seen as flowing directly from the ancient structure of the City of Lincoln.

The notion that cities are composed, like ecosystems, of basic types, which change slowly, but are flexible and adaptable, is being applied in the Foundation's work in town planning for historic town centres, including Lincoln. In his book *How Buildings Learn: What Happens After They Are Built*, American author Stewart Brand introduced the concept of pace layering, meaning that different parts of a building—or a city—change at different rates. When applied to civilisation, pace layering implies that certain deep structures, like the relationship between a city and nature, or the culture of a city, ought to change slowly, while other activities, like entertainment or retail, shift more quickly, and need to be accommodated in a flexible manner within these more permanent layers of the city.

We are beginning to understand that part of the problem in our cities is that we have been fundamentally altering basic underlying structures—the relation between the city and nature, movement patterns, the role of neighbourhoods in the city structure, the size of blocks—to accommodate short-term trends like retail packaging. A better understanding of the basic types that compose the city is needed in order to define ways to accommodate urban "fashions" like big-box retail in a flexible, and adaptable way.

When one looks at the recent history of planning, we are finding that contemporary planning interventions tend to alter the basic layers of the city for the sake of more transitory functions, such as retail trends or commercial needs. This is insane when one considers that retail exemplifies Schumpeter's idea of the creative destruction of capitalism, with merchandising trends succeeding one another at increasingly rapid rates. This trend of turning the layering upside down can fundamentally harm the basic functioning of the city by denying the reasons that it came to be in the first place. At the same time, far from being composed of basic adaptable types, recent development tends to be single purpose, functional, placeless and specific—and hence short lived.

When we looked at Lincoln during our workshops, we found that this was certainly the case, as the city centre had been altered dramatically in the past century and a half. First came the introduction of the railway at grade, severing the city centre from neighbourhoods to the South. Second came the imposition of grade-separated road systems creating further barriers, especially to the east and west. Recent developments of both government buildings and shopping centres have altered the basic structure of streets and pedestrian movement, walling off the river, hampering movement across the city and destroying continuity with a rich building tradition.

As all of these interventions reach the end of their useful life, the opportunity emerges to create an enduring framework for shaping the town centre that restores the ability to adapt flexibly to change while respecting the legacy of this ancient city. Such a legacy-driven framework can form the terms of a new partnership for managing change in Lincoln over time: between the resident of the city and its government, its cultural and social institutions and its landowners and commercial enterprises.

At its core, the town centre strategy for Lincoln, which emerged from intensive research and engagement with stakeholders, seeks to restore the balance in the city between nature, culture, government, movement and commerce. It consists of a series of interventions in the movement network and at key places in the city centre. When accomplished over a multi-year time frame, these interventions restore the basic circulatory system that gives life to the city and access to service, amenity and opportunity for its inhabitants, and set out a stable framework of building and road types that will enable the City of Lincoln to adapt and remain a principal urban centre for the Eastern Midlands into the foreseeable future.

Most importantly, the framework plan replaces the governing notion of planning intervention in the modern era—difference, and a conscious break with the past—with a new theme, continuity, with the built and natural legacy of the great cathedral city of Lincoln. This continuity can be expressed through each of Brand's themes:

Nature: The city centre master plan restores the ancient relationship between the city and the river by opening up access from the High Street to the Brayford Pool and the river, and by improving the quality of the public realm along the waterfront.

The relationship between the city on the river and the castle and cathedral on the top of the hill is reinforced both by making the pedestrian routes more legible, and by strengthening the vitality of the urban quarters in between.

Culture: The city centre plan seeks to enliven and connect the Cultural Quarter with the rest of the city, and to connect these attractions to the amenities in the Cathedral and the Castle. A legible route up the side of Steep Hill enables this loop.

Rather than seeking to define the cultural quarter through new landmark buildings, the plan celebrates the Lincoln Castle, where resides one of the surviving copies of the Magna Carta; the Cathedral, Steep Hill, with one of Britain's oldest extant houses; and the many bits of Roman legacy found throughout the "secret places" of ancient Lincoln.

Governance: The master plan seeks to create an enduring partnership for the custodianship of the Lincoln city centre, bringing together the City Council, the County Council and business and community interests in a project intended to ensure the health of the city centre for thirty years. Opportunity for private investment is unlocked by public "pump-priming," and private contributions fund key infrastructure.

Infrastructure: The damage done by transport interventions in the past 150 years to Lincoln's urban fabric had limited east–west connections across the city, severed the city north from south at the railway, and eliminated alternative north–south connections on either side of the city centre. The master plan repairs these rents in the urban fabric, and in the process reconnects the city's neighbourhoods to the beating heart of the city by restoring the integrity of the block structure in the centre.

Commerce: The functional approach to city planning has rendered most urban-core areas mono-cultural, devoted to shopping and perhaps office use, and little else. The introduction of a university to Lincoln has created another zone, and the cultural quarter has been viewed as a zone as well. The plan seeks to activate all of these single-use districts through the introduction of mixed-use strategies to create more diversified daytime as well as nighttime economies. For example, a project south of the railway station introduces higher-density residential and office uses into the city centre. People have always lived in the city centre, and it has always been a marketplace, a civic place and a sacred place, and the plan builds on this legacy.

Fashion: Retail centres brought to the core of the city have successfully maintained Lincoln as a substantial centre for shopping far in excess of its residential population, but this has also truncated the High Street, and tended to strangle circulation through the city centre. As these relatively recent centres age, there will be an opportunity to restructure retail so it can better compete by improving pedestrian and vehicular flow, and by better relating the various retail elements to one another. Retail can thus become a flexible part of a robust city structure.

A city that has endured for almost two thousand years ought to be planned so that it can continue to endure, and even to thrive. If a robust partnership can hold and champion this plan over that time, the result will be a city that can once again learn from its past, and apply those lessons to enable it to thrive and sustain into the future. The notions of legacy and continuity are central to the notion of sustainability, which is really about preserving choices for future generations. If we do so, whether with cities or by building sensitively in the context of historic buildings, we are preserving value and also enhancing value in new development. The idea of continuity runs contrary to current preservation dogma which stresses difference, and distinction—"the honestly modern"—but aligns closely with both common sense and thousands of years of building tradition.

Part 4. Bouquets and Brickbats

These pieces were written for a monthly column in the UK magazine Building Design, which has mostly covered issues of urbanism and housing. From time to time, though, I have strayed into criticism, which I have generally approached as an urbanist who cares about and appreciates buildings.

Part: Bouquets of Brickbats

London's Skyscraper Designers Should Aim High Like Chicago

Building Design

September 27, 2013

The decision by communities minister Eric Pickles to call in the Shell Centre surprised many, coming as it did after a period when it seemed like most anything goes in London. The action has been seen to reflect a growing disquiet over the cumulative impact of new large-scale development in the city, as much as it is a comment on the project itself.

And this, with the Walkie-Scorchie's antics, has turned up the heat on the long-simmering debate about tall buildings in London.

Debates over tall buildings often seem to come down to the impact on heritage, and more particularly on the view impact on World Heritage sites, in this case the Palace of Westminster. Issues of place-making, variety, density and context are inevitably less debated.

London predominantly achieves density through street-based urbanism of terraces and mansion blocks, with towers in the park serving as social housing. Canary Wharf was to be the place for high-rise development of the Singapore or Manhattan type, and until recently tall buildings elsewhere tended to be isolated examples of developer persuasiveness.

The London Plan calls for areas of concentrated development; the Shell Centre and nearby Elizabeth House are in one of these areas.

I attended university in Chicago, and this is where I learned to love both urbanism and architecture. Chicago is where the tall building first broke free from the limits of masonry, and the work of Burnham & Root, Holabird & Roche and Louis Sullivan is still worth learning from in terms of a tall-building quarter for London.

Sullivan famously used the classical column for his theory of a tripartite skyscraper design, with a base of two to four storeys for public functions, lobbies and retail addressing the pedestrian realm; the shaft, containing residences or offices; and the attic storey, terminating the building. Too often today, while people experience the city at the scale of the entrance, the street and the skyline, the entire building is conceived as one object.

Sullivan has been claimed as a proto-modernist for saying that form follows function, but he also said a building's identity derives from its ornament. The Shell Centre's buildings seem to follow the first precept, if the function is to deliver an efficient floorplate, but fail the second, offering an identity distinguished only by the varied sizes of the openings.

Many architects are starting to experiment with decoration and ornament, and it is a shame this hasn't been tried with a tall building.

The other function of any building is to help make a place, and to address the street. The redeveloped Shell Centre could have been London's Rockefeller Center, with a legible plan around central intersecting axes and a grand public space. Instead it feels as if the building floorplates defined the masterplan, of buildings on plots with passages in between. There are no clear axes, and the public square is not a central organising space.

The Shell Centre feels like a lost placemaking and architectural opportunity, with its prime location on the river and a listed building at the centre.

Sadly, the issues before the government seem to relate to view corridors, not the kind of city we are building.

An Urbanist's View of the Stirling Shortlist

Building Design

July 22, 2014

Last year's Stirling Prize was viewed by many as a move away from icons, and Astley Castle was seen as a surprisingly good choice.

This year, it appears the Stirling Prize shortlist is back to rewarding cultural and institutional buildings with large budgets. With one exception, all are buildings in infill contexts, and so I thought an evaluation of their urbanism might be instructive.

The flaneur's view of the city is more demanding of architecture than the motorist's, as the city unfolds at 5mph and in finer grain. Buildings frame and define the public realm, and good urban performance ought to be a prerequisite for a Stirling Prize winner. In addition to the core Vitruvian triad of commodity, firmness and delight, an urbanist might add how the building's base addresses the street, how legible the entrances are to the pedestrian, the relationship to the urban plan and whether detailing stands up to close scrutiny. Buildings may look great when seen while passing at 70mph or from atop Parliament Hill but be less successful when one walks up to them.

Of the Stirling shortlist, only the Aquatics Centre is an object in a park, and Zaha Hadid is gifted at such sculptural objects. The ground plane is replete with blank walls and shopping mall entrances with all the love reserved for the shapes above. To award it the Stirling would be to vaunt object-making over city- and place-making.

The Manchester College of Art by Feilden Clegg Bradley Studios tries the old trick of transparency through glass and ends up in a sort of category confusion as to whether it is an office building or an art school. For an art school, there is surprisingly little craft and no decoration, and so it doesn't get better the closer you get.

The Shard fails the urban test by overwhelming the light industrial streets in which it is set. It will, if fully occupied, add further stress to an overburdened public transport system and pavements in the area. But opprobrium ought really to be focused on the abysmal way the Shard meets the ground, with no inflection save that required for loading and unloading and with blank walls greeting the walker. While it may add interest to the skyline it is destructive at the ground plane, and surely we can require architects to respond to both scales?

The new Birmingham Library by Mecanoo is ballyhooed by its architect for responding to context in two ways: being on a walking desire line through the city and by utilising a tacky cladding over the glass boxes that is meant to evoke the city's jewellery-making heritage. Abstracting a metaphor to justify recycling a decorative motif that has naught to do with the buildings around stretches credulity. From a pedestrian perspective, the building is oppressive, the entrance is neither legible nor uplifting, and it fails utterly to relate to neighbouring buildings or the gardens across Cambridge Street.

The LSE student centre extension by O'Donnell & Tuomey is an infill building on a difficult site made more difficult by "right of light" limitations that, together with viewsheds, seem increasingly to dictate the shapes of London buildings. LSE has gradually expanded to occupy a neighbourhood and the centre is intended to provide a heart to the campus. It does so by framing a tiny plaza in front of the building and by opening up inside. This reminds us that Nolli's map of Rome showed not only the spaces made by streets and squares but also the enclosed public spaces. In scale and material, though not shape, the building fits in and the build quality is generally good, although one is surprised to see expansion joints on a £24 million building.

Haworth Tompkins's Everyman Theatre in Liverpool fits thoughtfully into the street and references the city's built heritage in material and form in a way that is neither slavish nor obscure. It embraces the pedestrian with a lively street frontage, broken into a bottom two storeys, a middle section and a roof scape, and it has an inviting and legible entrance. This is all common sense, yet so few bother. My only worry is that the decorative steel panels illustrating Liverpool residents may not age well, and one wonders how they will be viewed in a decade or 20 years' time.

If one were to award the Stirling solely on urban terms, I think the Everyman Theatre would win because it gives so much to the city and the street.

Don't Students Need Proper Housing?

Building Design

August 30, 2013

It is striking that two of the six shortlisted Carbuncle Cup projects are student accommodation. A look at this rapidly growing sector provides an insight into trends in property development globally, and is alarming for lovers of the city and of architecture.

Both the Caledonian Road scheme in Islington and the Castle Hill project blighting Port Meadow in Oxford reflect developers maximising profits by delivering a standardised product. At both projects this results in some true awfulness, as the "product" is adjusted badly to reflect actual conditions.

At Caledonian Road the retention of an historic facade by clamping it on front of the building without aligning the openings means a large proportion of units have obscured views and diminished daylight. The adaptation of the standard block at Castle Hill to make a gesture toward view protection results in strange roof profiles and awkward proportions.

Lots of student housing is being built—GVA counted planning applications in excess of 27,000 beds in the first eight months of 2012. This is being driven by strong overseas demand to study in the UK, and, importantly, by an appetite from investment funds. Savills has recently suggested there is a strong underlying demand for up to 266,000 more beds.

Student housing is now a commodity, with standard unit types and plans and a financial model that delivers a margin to the developer and to the downstream property fund that will buy and hold it. By and large, the sector is self-regulated, with a voluntary code calling for things that are generally covered in building regulations or health and safety. It seems to be felt that occupancy of less than a year and busy student lifestyles mean that standards can be reduced. For example, the Caledonian Road planning inspector found in favour of the project despite low daylighting levels, remarking that the rooms "would not be unacceptably oppressive within the context of the intended typical nature of occupation."

The banality of most of these buildings can make an impact on urban life in places like Holloway Road and Caledonian Road or Lincoln High Street. Most will not age well, and one doubts that they are adaptable to other uses should the overseas demand dry up.

Student buildings need not be blots on the landscape, and small units need not be oppressive. Universities like Oxford and Cambridge have long built gracious urban residences around courtyards; the contrast is what makes the Castle Hill scheme such a shocker.

Beautiful halls of residence can help to attract students. Swansea University has commissioned Hopkins and Porphyrios to design their new campus and residences, creating a new urban neighbourhood on Swansea Bay. Strong international universities like Oxford, Cambridge, Edinburgh, LSE and King's College should exercise similar leadership, insisting on good urban buildings that improve neighbourhoods, contribute to amenities and make contributions to affordable housing.

Such a commitment might help to attract students and differentiate their brands in a positive way, while adding diversity and vitality to urban life.

The Urbanist's Stirling Prize

Building Design

August 4, 2016

Once again the Stirling Prize shortlist is out, and once again one sees a varied lot of building typologies and approaches. Of course the House in Essex deserved to be on the list, but instead of beating that drum, I am going to look at the shortlist and rate them in terms of their response to their urban (or rural) context.

The Stirling trend seems to be towards rewarding worthiness—housing, schools and the like—and one hopes that one year the judges will award the building which best responds to its context. In the meantime, however, here are an urbanist's picks for the Stirling Prize.

The City of Glasgow College's Riverside campus by Michael Laird and Reiach & Hall deploys some of the old modernist tropes: a podium replete with pilotis, a ground level which seems aimed at cars and services and a colonnade facing the river. The acknowledgement of the presence of the river is notable in Glasgow, where riverside development has clunkily ignored it. There is a price to pay for this though, as there is no door on the street, and the user has to go all the way to the riverfront to enter through the colonnade.

OutHouse by Loyn & Co Architects is another one of those buildings that addresses its context by hiding within it. It is mostly underground, which is contextual in the way that some architects think putting a lawn on top of a building is green. The parts that do rise above the surface are concrete and wood and resolutely horizontal, surely pleasing the planners who would seek a low profile. But there is no reference to local building traditions or materials or to precedent in terms of standalone houses in a region of long settlement.

The Blavatnik School of Government by Hertzog & de Meuron is a building of great bravado in Oxford, a city filled with great architecture. It is determinedly anti-contextual, choosing instead to be a statement building that uses no stone, ignores the grammar of nearby buildings and stands apart from the street in a blaze of glazing. In front is a blank expanse of paving. The RIBA statement about the building argues that it enhances its neighbours by its difference and that it makes subtle references to its setting, but they are too subtle for me. I see only a glaring rejection.

Trafalgar Place by dRMM Architects is part of the controversial Elephant & Castle redevelopment. It responds to its context in terms of building materials, using brick for its facade. The building's street facade addresses the street in a workmanlike way with both planting, fenestration and legible entrances, and there is an internal pedestrian street which seems well enclosed and overlooked. The main building block height responds to the surrounding buildings while the two towers rise well above them.

The Weston Library by Wilkinson Eyre is primarily an inside job, repurposing a grade II-listed building by Giles Gilbert Scott. Kudos to RIBA for including it on the list and to Oxford University for giving it new life. The external intervention is largely to give the entrance more legibility and drama and as such it materially improves the urbanity of the building and the street.

It's no secret that I like the work of Caruso St John for its subtlety, its materiality and craft. The Newport Street Gallery is another triumph, and one which gets this urbanist's Stirling for 2016. The incorporation of new buildings alongside historic warehouses is done in a way that creates a coherent street facade, while showing that there are five separate buildings that make up the streetscape. This creates a pleasing rhythm on the street. As always with Caruso St John the choice of material fits both the context and the brief, and it is clear that the presentation of art in the internal galleries has not been subordinated to the architect's desire to make a statement building. It's a sturdy yet finely crafted building on a tough site.

All told most of this year's Stirling shortlist are at least making some urban gestures and at least half are doing a good job. That's good news for the flaneur.

Location Dictates the Success of Monument Design

Building Design
July 12, 2012

In June, I accompanied a friend on a trip to American Civil War battlegrounds and memorials in Washington, DC, and Virginia. A bit of a busman's holiday, it revealed the way that monuments and memorials engage with both history and landscape, and can add or detract from the experience of both.

I missed the opening of the Bomber Command memorial in Green Park, although the critical furore did cross the Atlantic. We arrived in DC to the news that Congress had stripped its funding of Frank Gehry's memorial to President Dwight D. Eisenhower, in the face of opposition from the Eisenhower family and others.

History is not simple, and most new monuments now become battlegrounds of their own. Our visit to Civil War sites showed that this contested nature is nothing new. Civil War commemoration expressed these conflicts through inscriptions, realistic sculpture and classical devices reflecting the differing positions. When well managed, these objects add meaning and beauty to an ordinary landscape that once saw extraordinary events. At the same time, the older memorials add a historical layer of their own, recalling the interpretations or design trends of an earlier time. When done poorly or in too great a number, they add up to a kind of grandiose litter, overwhelming the landscape and obscuring the event.

Washington, DC, is overwhelmingly neoclassical, and major monuments to Jefferson, Lincoln and Washington are focal points in the plan and visitor experience. Alongside these stand many statues and monuments in squares and circles. Of the modern monuments, Maya Lin's minimalist Vietnam Veterans Memorial is most successful, in its modesty, formality and power.

The Eisenhower memorial proposal is the latest, occupying a six-acre site at the edge of the Mall. The huge scale contradicts the essential modesty of Eisenhower, while its depiction of Eisenhower simultaneously demeans him by stressing his humble origins. Gehry has placed his massive objects in a formal manner, yet without detail they appear crude and bombastic. One rather longs for a statue of Ike on a jeep!

Memorials can be a kind of grandiose litter
For the Bomber Command, Liam O'Connor has used classical language to dignify the sacrifice of the bomber crews while enclosing the edge of Green Park. It conveys nuance through the creation of contemplative space, a plan that leads to and encloses that space and the use of formal language. The reaction against it has been more about the politics of bombing civilian populations than about the 55,000 bomber crew casualties, and reflexively, of course, reignited the style wars.

O'Connor's design for the National Memorial Arboretum in Staffordshire evoked little of the controversy of the Bomber Command memorial, although it used the same restrained classicism. Perhaps this is a sign that these kind of memorials should be placed outside the capital city and its monumental core, and also that the style wars are less vituperative outside the M25. Although interest groups will dislike being ejected from London or Washington, DC, locating future memorials at places of significance outside the capital cities could boost tourism and preserve the Royal Parks for future generations.

It's Time for a New Serpentine Design Brief

Building Design

May 18, 2012

It would be hard to invent the story that has unfolded around the Serpentine pavilion's chosen superstars for 2012, Herzog & de Meuron and Ai Weiwei, and their proposal to excavate and interpret the lost foundations of the previous dozen pavilions. The discovery that the previous pavilions lacked foundations—or that the foundations had been removed—means that the designers are free to make up their own story about the previous structures. And the idea that their structure will be a disc upon which people can reflect their own desires—through dance or whatever—perfectly reflects the disengagement between the architecture of spectacle and meaning. One suspects that the story is playing out just as Ai Weiwei would have liked.

I have generally found the annual Serpentine circus, along with the Biennale, to be the most satisfying foray into modern starchitecture. The limited budget and the temporary nature force a degree of engagement with the place that exceeds that found in many permanent buildings. When the lead guitarists of architecture turn their attention to corporate offices or major cultural projects the results are striking, but often sit uneasily with neighbouring buildings, or treat the street and the pedestrian with contempt.

Temporary pavilions in the park get to dodge all those issues. In my more misanthropic moments I have wished that many contemporary buildings by the superstars had been limited to being temporary constructions or architectural models in cultural venues.

The Serpentine pavilion has famously had an open brief for the past dozen years—apart from the designer having not built in England before (Herzog & de Meuron are saved by the collaboration with Ai Weiwei), the site, and the temporary nature of the project.

If as Jacques Herzog said, "almost everything has been done," and the appropriate response is to reflect on the non-existent foundations of prior pavilions, then maybe it's time for a new brief. After all, the era of the icon may be in decline in these times of restraint, reuse and budgetary constraint.

Instead of asking a superstar to surprise us, we could challenge each designer to build something well, beautifully and make it useful. Perhaps the pavilion should have a next use, and be designed to be installed somewhere else, in a park or a garden or a square. Maybe an architect from the traditional side of the spectrum could be invited, like Robert Stern, Hans Kollhoff or Rob Krier, none of whom have built in this country.

Or—and this is my preference—the Serpentine Gallery could dispense with the rock stars altogether, and ask a different group of students to design and build each year. There are an increasing number of student-build projects including our own at The Prince's Foundation, the Centre for Alternative Technology in Wales, and Design & Make at the AA. A high-profile design-build project at the Serpentine Gallery could stimulate practical teaching in architecture. If one coupled it with criteria about the provenance of materials, sustainability and reuse, it could give the Serpentine pavilion a new lease of life.

Part 5: Sustainability and Tradition

Sustainability is one of those words that has been so used and abused that it has become almost meaningless. This long piece attempts to recover its original meaning as the thread that binds past and future generations, exploring the role of both tradition and innovation in building in a way that lasts, while not foreclosing options for our children and grandchildren.

At the heart of this notion is the idea of living together in cities, towns and villages in community.

Sustainability and Tradition

Sustainability has come to be associated with cutting-edge technology, and in architecture, with glass, steel, solar panels, and wind turbines. Most images of proposed eco cities feature moody art direction inspired by the film "Blade Runner," and buildings derived from the "high-tech" modernism of the two British architectural lords Richard Rogers and Norman Foster. In fact, a recent study found that 79 percent of Britons surveyed viewed sustainable housing as being associated with the term "high-tech" and over 90 percent viewed sustainable housing as "modern" rather than "old-fashioned."

Americans overwhelmingly look to technology for sustainability as well, with the Harris Poll finding that 67 percent of those surveyed favored technology applications to produce "green products and services."

A second, smaller strand of thought views sustainability as being associated with the "less is more," "back to the land" movements of the sixties and seventies. This Hobbit Green, as opposed to high-tech green, features homes called "earth ships," made of tires and built largely underground, and a do-it-yourself aesthetic. A small but growing movement for co-housing—jointly owned housing developments with shared kitchens and common areas—in the United States exemplifies this trend. In the UK, the Transition Town movement, championed by Rob Hopkins and pioneered by the town of Totnes, looks to a local economy, local money and a dramatically reduced ecological footprint through voluntary local association.

The problem with both the high-tech vision and with Hobbit Green is that, by and large, consumers want to live in a traditional house with modern conveniences in a traditional setting and work in a traditional office building. Surveys in both the US and the UK typically show that a large majority of consumers prefer to live in traditional homes.

If the only routes to sustainability are the Buck Rogers and the Hobbit routes, then consumers will find themselves left out. Clearly, if sustainability and high-technology style are viewed as linked in the eyes of consumers, and consumers prefer traditional settings, it will be harder to get them to adopt sustainable practices in the built environment. At the same time, tradition is viewed with scorn among built-environment professionals, derided as kitsch and as pastiche, resulting in a disconnect between the professionals and their clients. As T. S. Eliot remarked of tradition as far back as 1922, "Seldom does the word appear except in a phrase of censure. If otherwise, it is vaguely approbative, with the implication . . . of some pleasing archaeological reconstruction."

If tradition and the vernacular have much to teach us about sustainability, and in fact can serve as the base from which to evolve cities, towns and buildings that can respond to our global environmental challenges, then resolving this seeming conflict is as much a matter of better social marketing as anything else. Perhaps the answers have been right under our nose the whole time, if we look past the last fifty years of planning and architectural trends to the deeper patterns that underlie human settlement on the planet over a few thousand years.

Resolving this conflict will require better definitions of both sustainability and tradition, and the re-establishment of living traditions, which evolve to confront contemporary challenges.

In defining sustainability, it is useful to go right back to the origins of the term, with the United Nations Brundtland Commission in 1987. "Sustainable development is development that meets the needs of the present without compromising the ability of future generations to meet their own needs."

The Commission was charged with reconciling the challenge of a developing world with the natural environment, and their definition above clearly placed sustainability in an intergenerational and a global context. The challenges of the present day must be resolved in a way that does not reduce choices for future generations. The Brundtland Commission recognized two key concepts: the notion that there must be limits in the present day, and the notion that a global commons extends to future generations as well.

Since the 1987 report, the notion of sustainability has been widely embraced, and has been viewed as having three interrelated components: environment, equity and economy. This three-pronged approach was taken up in the US by the President's Council on Sustainable Development, an initiative of the Clinton Administration championed by then-Vice President Al Gore. Each of the three sectors has since argued that their sector is most important, and that it is getting short shrift; and as a result, the core notion of a compact between generations has tended to be lost.

At the same time, this has led to a concept of sustainability as being essentially the domain of technical people, who will manage a set of inputs and outputs on a global scale balancing the three sectors in a sort of big black box. This can be contrasted to the ecological approach to sustainability, which sees it as being rooted in culture and its adaptation to place. This notion of a human ecology of sustainability was developed by David Orr in his book *The Nature of Design*:

> Settled cultures, without using the word 'ecology', have designed with ecology in mind because to do otherwise would bring ruin, famine and social disintegration. Out of necessity they created harmony between intentions and the genius of particular places that preserved diversity of both natural and biological capital; utilized current solar income, created little or no waste, imposed few unaccounted costs and supported cultural and social patterns.

This notion of an ecological approach to design incorporates the intergenerational idea of linking present with future embodied in the Brundtland Commission's definition of sustainable development, embraces the notion of limiting growth to the use of natural and human capital, and introduces the notion of rootedness in place, habitat and culture. Perhaps most importantly, it restores to the idea of sustainability the link idea that we can learn from past generations as well as from present technology. This brings us to the idea of tradition.

T.S. Eliot writes of tradition in "Tradition and the Individual Talent:"

"Yet if the only form of tradition, of handing down, consisted in following the ways of the immediate generation before us in a blind or timid adherence to its successes, 'tradition' should positively be discouraged.... This historical sense, which is a sense of the timeless as well as of the temporal and of the timeless and of the temporal together, is what makes a writer traditional."

Traditional thinking is often derided as romanticism, and as historicism, largely because of the influence of the modern movement. History is seen as a succession of movements, with the Enlightenment and the Industrial Revolution having been succeeded in the twentieth century by the modernist movement. In the arts, architecture and in philosophy, a foundational belief of modernism is the idea of a "courageous break with the past, and...the machine-age in all its implications: new materials, new processes, new forms, new problems."

Architects such as Le Corbusier defined the city and the building as "machines for living," and called for "a concord between men and machines." The idea that the past was irrelevant to modern problems has become engrained in teaching, especially in schools of architecture, and tradition and vernacular have become objects of historical study, rather than representing living processes. The rejection of tradition was linked to the creation of a series of new technology-driven building processes, all propelled by the idea of a machine age based upon fossil fuels and industrial production systems: freeways and motorways; the separation of city circulation into motorized and pedestrian zones; single-use zoning of the city into housing districts, shopping centers, office and business parks, and leisure zones; suburban tract housing; the "curtain wall" and the "balloon frame;" and a host of other innovations. The failure of many of these untested planning and design ideas is not surprising, nor is their inability to evolve to confront new ecological realities such as higher fuel prices or climate change.

In the meantime, traditional neighborhoods, streets and buildings have quietly continued to evolve and go through cycles of decay, renewal and rebirth as the long-term value of long-lived places continues to endure. In a study for The Prince's Foundation and the British Property Federation, the consulting firm Savills studied three conventional suburban developments, three "new urban" developments and three historic neighborhoods, in similar market areas. The conventional projects displayed the lowest appreciation in prices over time; the "new urban" developments the second best performance; and in every case, the historic neighborhoods displayed the greatest price appreciation.

Webster's Dictionary describes tradition as "a long established custom or practice." Surely part of the problem in architecture and planning is that the modernist movement has disrupted the custom and practice of tradition, by decreeing the past to be irrelevant. At least three generations of architects and planners have graduated from school without studying traditional architecture or urban design as a living practice, and this means that living traditional architects and urban planners are either self-taught or learned through informal apprenticeship. The situation in traditional building crafts is hardly better, with schools of traditional building only lately being established in Charleston and in the UK. There is only one university architecture school offering even a traditional architecture studio in the United Kingdom, and only a few which tolerate students that are interested in the subject. The situation is a bit better in the United States, where at least three schools are dedicated to traditional architecture and urbanism, and a number teach it as part of a balanced architectural education.

Traditional architecture and urbanism are alive and well, however, in cities, towns and villages across the world, and the close study of successful precedents has been a fruitful way of learning to make new places that also work. Both the American new urbanists and the British traditional urbanists have built a large body of evidence from the documentation of typology of streets, squares, blocks and buildings, and have gradually learned to apply the principles learned from this study to make new places that go beyond the copying of historic styles. At both the scale of the city and the scale of the building, the challenge is now one of evolving tradition to confront new challenges, including the rapid pace of development in a post-industrial, urbanizing world.

The environmental tradition has historically been about embracing and preserving the natural places, and environmentalists have often viewed cities as dirty, polluting, unfortunate blights. This tendency to place nature and man in opposition derives from both the popular rejection of the Victorian city and its polluting factories and foul sewers, and from the roots of environmentalism in saving threatened species and preserving habitat and scenic beauty.

Environmentalists responded by regulating industrial and urban discharge into water and air, through planning laws to preserve countryside and reclaim industrial land, and through preserving and conserving farmland and wild places as green lungs for the planet. At the same time, however, the huge growth in global population, and the move from subsistence and market farming to industrial agriculture have together brought about an urban explosion, and cities have become a dominant feature in both the human and natural environment.

A few facts will help to make the needed connections. Despite its self-image as a nation of villagers, the United Kingdom population is overwhelmingly urban, with ninety percent living in urban places, according to the United Nations. The population of the United States is similarly concentrated in metropolitan areas. In 2007, Earth officially became an urban planet, with over half of the world's population living in cities. Globally, the twenty-first century will be the urban century. According to the United Nations Environment Programme, of the global population increase of 2.2 billion by 2030, 2.1 billion will live in urban areas; and by 2030, over sixty percent of the world's population will be urban dwellers.

Two issues arise here. First, if all these urban dwellers adopt the suburban living patterns and lifestyles of the United States and Western Europe, the climate problem will be greatly exacerbated. Second, many—if not most—of the new urban dwellers in the Southern Hemisphere live in grossly overcrowded slums, rife with cholera and other diseases, and where infant mortality, malnutrition and lack of secure land tenure are endemic problems. These slums may be environmentally sustainable, but only because their residents have next to nothing.

Global urbanization is thus both a social and environmental issue, and the challenge of raising global living standards while reducing carbon emissions is a knotty problem. By and large, then, this trend toward global urbanization is seen as a problem worldwide—for all of the traditional reasons about pollution and overcrowding, plus challenges of public health, nutrition and engagement in civil society.

People all over the world are moving to cities for a reason, and that reason is that cities are seen as offering the opportunity for a better life because they provide the chance for employment, training, access to health care, to education and to the online world. In other words, cities are efficient places for humans, and increasingly are key to a successful human ecology. For when we look at urban places, we find not only solutions to the personal transport part of the climate problem—density, connected streets, accessible public transport, more efficient buildings and mixed use—but also solutions for the broader social challenge of truly sustainable development.

Thinking of cities as habitat for humans (and songbirds, insects and small mammals!) means organizing cities in ways that offer different choices in our day-to-day lives: greener ways of living, of moving around—or not having to move around so much—of delivering food and services.

Responding to the urgent crises of climate change is often seen as a burden, and as a threat. People fear that life in the future will be more limited, and that being green means making sacrifices. That's not necessarily so. The shift to green, resource-efficient cities could well add to quality of life, and in fact people might eat better, be healthier and have just as many choices as before. They will just be different choices!

The fundamental premise is that thinking of cities as artifacts of natural processes might inform the way we plan and design. Cities might be planned to evolve organically, rather than in a mechanical fashion. What are the implications of such an approach for the quality of people's lives?

First, we might begin by defining the properties of healthy ecosystems, and look to apply those properties to the conscious process of city-making. A series of attributes emerge from the study of complex systems: basic typologies, which change slowly but are highly flexible and adaptable; built-in redundancy as a way of ensuring reliability;

and feedback loops as a way of responding to change. Anthropologist and systems theorist Gregory Bateson called for "a single system of environment combined with high human civilization, in which the flexibility of the civilization shall match that of the environment to create an ongoing complex system, open-ended for slow change of even basic characteristics."

The notion that cities are composed, like ecosystems, of basic types, which change slowly but are flexible and adaptable, is being applied in the Foundation's work in town planning for historic town centers. In his book, *How Buildings Learn,* American author and deep-green thinker Stewart Brand introduced the concept of "pace layering," meaning that different parts of a building—or a city—change at different rates.

The slow layers are meant to be most adaptable and longest-lived, while the fast layers respond and change quickly. Nature is a fundamental layer of civilization, meant to change most slowly, while fashion skims the surface, changing by vagary and whim. When this idea is applied to city planning, we begin to develop a new sense of priorities, acting as steward for nature, and accommodating short-term trends like retail formats and commerce within the flexible fabric of the urban structure rather than altering fundamental structures to adjust to them.

Scale means understanding the role of buildings, streets, neighbourhoods, towns and regions in a complex system. Regions are about the interaction of complex systems: markets, institutions that regulate them, and the transport that creates access to them. Regions are made up of a system of walkable neighbourhoods, interconnected by streets and transport networks, each serving its own function.

Scale makes it possible to efficiently operate public transport systems, providing a meaningful alternative to the automobile. Scale also allows the provision of environmental infrastructure such as sustainable urban drainage or combined heat and power that are more cost effective at the neighborhood or district level.

An interconnected street network provides for a better distribution of traffic, lessening congestion on major roads. The avoidance of "wiggly worm" cul-de-sacs allows for the creation of walkable neighbourhoods that accommodate the automobile but celebrate the pedestrian.

A mixed community is built around the form of streets, blocks and buildings, and the types of buildings rather than type of land use. It allows for employment and retail within close proximity of residences.

Mixed communities also provide a range of housing types and sizes, accommodating affordable housing through "pepper potting" rather than in monocultural, disconnected estates.

These characteristics add up to something called location efficiency. Location efficiency, which can be quantified, is the combination of greater residential density, increased pedestrian and bicycle friendliness and access to public transport. Improved location efficiency results in reduced vehicle travel, lower carbon emissions and reduced household transportation expenses.

If we look at cities and towns in terms of per-capita environmental burden, rather than on an area-wide basis, they are far more environmentally friendly than sprawling suburbs. On a per-square-mile basis, city centers seem far dirtier than the suburbs and farmland, because of the concentration of roads and cars and buildings.

When one recalculates on a per-capita basis, a very different story emerges: on a per-capita basis, city centers contribute much less carbon than do suburban areas. The combination of scale, density, street connectivity and mixed community makes all the difference.

To test this in Britain, The Prince's Foundation for the Built Environment, with partners including the Center for Neighborhood Technology, Space Syntax, and Seth Harry Associates, undertook a master plan for the highly accessible London suburban town center of Walthamstow, seeking to increase the stock of affordable housing, improve accessibility, safety and the retail offer, and reduce per-capita carbon emissions at the same time. Through a unique participatory design process called Enquiry by Design, the Foundation worked with local authorities, residents and businesses to create a master plan that preserved existing neighborhood character filled in with mid-rise, mixed-use development based on historic building types, improved walkable access to the town center and public transport, and proposed the reorientation of public transport routes in the center.

The resulting plan accommodated over 2,400 new residences while reducing carbon emissions from vehicle travel by three tons per household per annum. It was supported by two-thirds of residents surveyed and has been adopted by the London Borough of Waltham Forest.

The combination of a grounding in traditional urban patterns and building typologies, engagement with community in order to tap into local intelligence, and the use of evidence-based tools like the location efficiency model and space syntax methodology move the Walthamstow project from traditional urbanism to sustainable urbanism.

Residential densities allowing for exchange, interconnected street patterns, public transport systems and mixed use are characteristics of traditional urban communities, and properly designing for sustainability means being grounded in an ever-evolving tradition. If one views tradition rather than self-conscious newness as a foundation for sustainability, then the challenge is one of reconnecting with adaptation to place, and employing new evidence-based tools for evolving applicable precedents to confront and solve new challenges.

Two examples of this approach come from The Prince's Foundation's master planning work at Lincoln and at Romsey in Hampshire. Lincoln, where The Prince's Foundation was asked to develop a new master plan for the city center, is very different from the essentially Victorian London suburb of Walthamstow. The Romans founded the city over 2,000 years ago, and the challenge at Lincoln is to find a way to repair the damage to its physical environment, accessibility and sense of community from the past century of industrialization, motorization and inward-facing shopping centers.

Stewart Brand's thinking about rates of change helped us at Lincoln, providing a sustainability tool for unpacking the changes over time. The work of the master planner is placed in the context of nature, culture, governance, infrastructure, commerce, and fashion. With nature the role of the planner is one of stewardship, and with culture one of sustaining, rather than a more active role. The master planner stands in for governance in this case, mediating the need to maintain and husband cultural and ecological resources against the demands of the present; for infrastructure, which has shaped communities; for commerce, which must be accommodated; and for fashion, the fastest-changing—think about window displays or mobile-phone stores—which should be absorbed.

When we looked at Lincoln during our workshops, we found that this was certainly the case, as the city center had been altered dramatically in the past century and a half. First came the introduction of the railway at grade, severing the city center from neighborhoods to the south.

Second came the imposition of grade-separated road systems creating further barriers, especially to the east and west. Recent developments of both government buildings and shopping centers have altered the basic structure of streets and pedestrian movement, walling off the river, hampering movement across the city, and destroying continuity with a rich building tradition.

As all of these interventions reach the end of their useful life, the opportunity emerges to create an enduring framework for shaping the town center that restores the ability to adapt flexibly to change while respecting the legacy of this ancient city. At its core, the town center strategy for Lincoln, which emerged from intensive research and engagement with stakeholders, consists in a series of interventions in the transportation network and at key places in the city center. When accomplished over a multi-year time frame, these interventions restore the basic circulatory system that gives life to the city and access to service, amenities and opportunity for its inhabitants, and sets out a stable framework of building and road types that will enable the City of Lincoln to adapt and remain a principal urban center for the Eastern Midlands into the foreseeable future.

Most importantly, the framework plan replaces the governing notion of planning intervention in the modern era—difference, and a conscious break with the past—with a new theme of continuity with the built and natural legacy of the great cathedral city of Lincoln. A city that has endured for almost two thousand years ought to be planned so that it can continue to endure, and even to thrive. If a robust partnership can hold and champion this plan over that time, the result will be a city that can once again learn from its past, and apply those lessons to enable it to thrive and sustain into the future. The idea of continuity runs contrary to current preservation dogma, which stresses difference and distinction—"the honestly modern"—but aligns closely with both common sense and thousands of years of building tradition.

A major problem with twentieth-century urban and suburban development has been the way that it has dealt with storm water and drainage through channelization and underground pipes and culverts. This engineering approach to drainage has tended to create downstream problems of flooding and water-quality problems, and it has reduced the ability of aquifers to recharge naturally. As a result, in recent years, engineers have begun to try to evolve sustainable urban drainage techniques that reduce the amount of impervious surfaces in new development and attempt to handle storm water on site through infiltration into ground water and through detention basins that delay discharge into stream systems. The engineering solutions have been intended solely to deal with stormwater issues, and when imposed into urban plans, tend to break up the pattern of walkable blocks, create large "no-go" areas, and impose large concrete structures into roadsides and residential neighborhoods—a typical result of single-order solutions, which do not deal with the complexity of urban environments.

At Upton in Northamptonshire, where The Prince's Foundation and EDAW worked with the local borough and English Partnerships to master plan an urban extension to the town of 5,000 residences, flooding downstream in the River Nene was always a key issue. As a result, sustainable drainage was integrated into the scheme from the outset, with the goal of doing so in a way that worked well with the creation of walkable, human-scaled streets and the creation of a pleasant green network of public spaces. The sustainable drainage swales were integrated into the street sections in a way that is properly enclosed and well landscaped, making a scenic virtue of a sustainability necessity.

In all of these examples, the Foundation employs a three-stage design process, beginning with a grounding in traditional urbanism, seeking to understand how it has been adapted in a place through time and response to local conditions, economy and geography, and then evolving it using a series of evidence-based design tools to refine the developing master plan. The Foundation does all of this in the place in which it is working, utilizing the Enquiry by Design methodology to engage expert stakeholders in an interdisciplinary enquiry, tap into community concerns and local intelligence and move between scales to consider the whole along with the parts.

At the scale of the city, the town and the neighborhood, it is clear that traditional urbanism can be demonstrated to have profound sustainability implications, and that the process of evolving traditional urban patterns to confront today's sustainability challenges is well underway. Just as clearly, centuries of vernacular and traditional building have much to teach us about how to live within our limits. But does tradition provide a platform for dealing with the very real problems of rapid global urbanization?

First, sustainability means building for the long term—one hundred years, rather than twenty years. Sustainability, as the Brundtland Commission defined it, is about making choices today that preserve choices for future generations—and that is also about creating a link through from the past by understanding what tradition has to teach us, then adapting it for present needs to make something that will be successful in a hundred years.

Because of this need for long-term thinking, it is essential to build in an adaptable, flexible and resilient manner, reassessing and reusing existing buildings wherever possible and making new buildings and neighborhoods that can learn. In the words of Stewart Brand, "The immediate program is not the generator, as the building should be designed to evolve, changing use over time as the user and the city around it may require."

Third, it means building in a manner that fits the place, in terms of materials used, proportion and layout, and climate, ecology and building practices. Instead of architecture as a global brand, what's needed is globalism from the bottom up, a design practice that enables local places to compete globally on the basis of distinctive character, local identity and place.

Fourth, it means building beautifully, in a manner that builds upon tradition, evolving it in response to present challenges and utilizing the best and most appropriate new technologies and techniques. Beautiful buildings can be defined simply, as buildings that are loved, and because they are loved, they will be cared for, be renewed, and be sustainable as a result.

Fifth, it means understanding the purpose of a building or group of buildings within the hierarchy of the buildings around it and responding with an appropriate building type and design. Doing this often implies composition of a harmonious whole, rather than the erection of singular objects of architectural or corporate will. In the city, most buildings are background buildings that stand as part of a composition, not singular objects, and could draw their character more from their neighbors than from the singular vision of the designer or client.

Finally, understanding that the role of the designer in this world crisis is less an act of creation and more the craft of marrying skills with local intelligence through community engagement, deep understanding of local identity and character, and the knowledge that most of the time what is required are background buildings.

It is worth noting that all of The Prince's Foundation's work in sustainable architecture is grounded in a sustainability process that begins with the application of a set of general principles (those outlined above), and proceeds to a deep study of local precedent and adaptation both through study on the ground and engagement with local communities, and then to a review of key challenges and the assessment and integration of appropriate new technologies, materials and tools. In this way sustainability and tradition are evolved in a way that both resonates with culture and place and takes it forward into the future.

His Royal Highness The Prince of Wales, founder of The Prince's Foundation for the Built Environment and, more recently, The Prince's Rainforest Project, has campaigned for decades on sustainability issues. He received the Vincent Scully Prize from the US National Building Museum for his contribution to architectural and urban practice, theory and criticism. In his acceptance speech, he called for a union of tradition and modernity, beyond the tyranny of "traditionalism" or "modernism."

To find new solutions for these major global issues it is essential that we combine a thorough understanding of how past civilizations ordered themselves, using minimal resources, together with new science and technologies so that we really can have our "cake and eat it." Modernism has led us to seek answers in a host of technical "fixes." Traditionalism often only pays it lip service. Real traditional thinking has always tried to see the whole picture.

This transformation will be profound and will involve much more than merely grafting green buildings and smart growth onto new urbanism in an opportunistic way. The opportunity of thinking in an integrated fashion about food, materials, energy and water alongside social issues such as employment, mixed housing, local identity, culture and governance is the opportunity for a new kind of globalism from the bottom up. Such a globalism would recognize the responsibility for sustainable development but realize it in a fashion "unique to local history, climate, ecology and building practice," achieving the blending of sustainability and tradition called for in this volume.

Part 6.
On Christopher Alexander's Athena Award

The architect and thinker Christopher Alexander changed my life. His work, along with that of Jane Jacobs and the anthropologists Gregory Bateson and Edward T. Hall, gave me a framework for reconciling the dissonance between what I saw and liked in cities and landscape and what I was being taught in school. I have relied on that intellectual framework ever since. It was a huge honor to present him with an award in 2006.

Presentation of the Athena Medal to Professor Christopher Alexander, Providence, Rhode Island, June 3, 2006

Good morning and thank you all for getting up early for what promises to be a very stimulating day in Providence. This morning I have the distinct honor of inaugurating, along with Andres Duany on Sunday, the first presentation of the Congress for the New Urbanism's Athena Awards.

The medal itself, designed and stamped in the manner of an ancient coin, is intended to be a timeless commemoration of the importance of a set of key individuals to the movement. Made by a ninety-year-old sculptor, the medal depicts Athena on one side, and an owl on the other.

These new awards are intended to recognize the pioneers of our movement, those who opened the door through which the founders and the signers of the Charter for the New Urbanism walked. Athena award winners, and there will be a fixed number of them over the next several years, are the individuals who first broke the stranglehold that ideological modernism had on architectural and planning thinking. They are the people who laid the intellectual groundwork for a more participatory, integrated approach to the city and the public realm.

These honorees are not the new urbanists, and indeed most of them still would not call themselves new urbanists. Instead, recipients of the Athena medal are the advance troops, who laid down the first critique, provided the theoretical underpinnings, or created the perceptual space that allowed the reform movement called New Urbanism to grow.

The medalists are not responsible for our mistakes or our successes. Without the Athena medalists, our movement might not have emerged. In this moment of growth for the CNU, this moment when a next generation is emerging to follow and challenge the founders, it is important to remember and recognize upon whose shoulders we stand, and to celebrate their work to date, and the work they continue to do. For these people still challenge us to do better.

It is a great privilege to have the opportunity to say some words of appreciation about the work of Christopher Alexander, as he has not only been a great influence on New Urbanism, but has had much affected my own thinking over the past twenty-five years.

I discovered *A Pattern Language* as a graduate student in 1979, as I was trying to find my place between an object-oriented architecture school and a regulation-obsessed planning school. As someone who had lived in the Chicago area throughout university, I had been exposed to the failings of urban renewal, which we called urban removal, to the way that freeways were used to divide and segregate and to the powerfully bad effect that high-rise public housing had on communities. All of these acts of planning and urban design were profoundly disturbing and alienating.

In short I was primed. Like most young people who came up in the 1970s, I had been transformed by the environmental movement and by the ideas of ecology and ecosystems, and though I found doses of Le Corbusier strangely invigorating, somehow I doubted in the machine analogy, and had been taught by Rachel Carson to disbelieve the notion that technology could save us.

Above all, I was experiencing profound moments of cognitive dissonance, reading these tremendously stirring calls to battle by urban reformers, and modernists, and finding the built products unsettling and infinitely less harmonious or comfortable than older neighborhoods of Chicago and Evanston where I went to university, or the classrooms designed by Cass Gilbert at the University of Texas where I was imbibing these heady thoughts of the new order and the future.

When I chanced upon *A Pattern Language*, it was a transformative moment, causing me to drop my thesis project, and to try to undertake a project to design a whole-systems approach to public engagement and community participation that embodied the pattern language. So the intellectual debt I owe to Christopher Alexander is profound, and to him I owe three core ideas that have permeated my own work ever since:

- The city is a complexly layered system, and human systems that try to reduce these patterns of interaction to a hierarchical system of collection and distribution are inherently destroying the complexity that makes the city a place of creativity and life. Hence my twenty-five year campaign against the functional classification system of the highway engineers!
- To paraphrase Korzybiski, who said "The map is not the territory," Alexander has taught me that the plan is not the project, and that it is the process of interactions between the plan and the community, the regulatory system, the financial system, the other professions, and the trades and contractors that makes the project.
- And finally, and most importantly, Christopher Alexander teaches that at the heart of making place is seeing, and understanding the things that touch us in nature, in our houses and in our cities, and not being afraid to trust our senses, and our emotions. In a hyper-rational world, Christopher Alexander has provided an opening to look at questions of quality, of ease of comfort and of beauty, and in aligning these ideas with nature, and with a series of principles in *The Nature of Order*, he has begun to provide us with some tools for thinking about imbedding these qualities in our work.

Alexander was elected fellow of the American Academy of Arts and Sciences in 1996, is a fellow of the Swedish Royal Society, has been the recipient of innumerable architectural prizes and honors including the gold medal for research of the American Institute of Architects, awarded in 1970.

He was raised in England, and holds a master's degree in Mathematics and a bachelor's degree in Architecture from Cambridge University, and a PhD in Architecture from Harvard University.

In 1958, he moved to the United States, and lived in Berkeley, California from 1963 until the moved to England several years ago. In Berkeley, he was professor of architecture at the University of California Berkeley and president of the Center for Environmental Structure.

Professor Alexander is a licensed contractor. He has built over 200 buildings on virtually all the continents, ranging from schools to houses to public facilities. His work on patterns has been enormously influential in the software world, inspiring the whole field of object-oriented programming.

His books include *A Pattern Language*, *The Timeless Way of Building*, *A New Theory of Urban Design*, *The Oregon Experiment*, and the four-volume series *The Nature of Order*. His website, livinglanguage.com, depicts his next effort—the creation of a process of unfolding through generative codes.

Why is this important to new urbanists, and why have we asked him to come before us and talk about his work, which is difficult philosophically and even epistemologically, at this Congress which is about implementing the New Urbanism, which focuses on the hard practicalities of the development process?

After all, *The Nature of Order* is about some concepts that are as profoundly unsettling today as *A Pattern Language* was 28 years ago: the idea that inanimate objects like buildings and carpets can embody life, the insight that we must create processes for building that unfold and generate over time, the insight that building places that work for the long haul involves doing things in close proximity with the land, with ordinary people and in a certain order, and finally that we've got almost all of those things wrong in the conventional process today.

In short, Chris Alexander's work challenges new urbanists by suggesting that seeking to engage as we do with the existing processes of production and modify them through the creation of new tools and systems may be insufficient. For example, charrettes, as important as they have been in moving toward collective participatory process, may not be the end point.

The Nature of Order implies that the very ways that we finance and build are antithetical to creating places that will evolve organically over time, and so on.

All this may be very hard to swallow. Aren't we on the cusp of some very profound changes as a movement? Hasn't the past decade and a half of struggle been hard enough?

But we all know that as we peel back one layer of the onion, we find another layer, and that as we gradually begin to replace use-based zoning or road standards, we find that short-term financing and contracting processes inhibit us. It is rather like pulling on a loose thread on a sweater, it's probably not going to be possible to stop.

In looking deeply at systems in nature and society, and at human aspirations and needs and in challenging us to understand that improved methodologies for urban design are not enough, Christopher Alexander is asking us to keep the eye on the prize: the creation of enduring, organic places that can grow and deepen in complexity and character over time.

In some very enjoyable conversations with Chris and Maggie Moore leading up to today, Maggie and Chris quite gently probed me about the direction of the CNU, and how we saw the infrastructure we had developed—charrettes, smart codes, regional visioning processes, pattern books and the like—and then reminded me of the profound aspirations of the Charter of the New Urbanism and, particularly, its preamble. And therein lies the reason why people like Chris and Leon Krier are so important to us.

We are a practical set of reformers, composed of practitioners, who must engage in the world as it is, making improvements a bit at a time and building systems and tools that, at the end of the day, have to be grafted onto an existing system.

But the Charter, like the Declaration of Independence, is a lofty document, describing aspirations and an end state that cannot be reached in a short period of time, or with the tools we have, or even the ones we have developed to date. Surely the underlying tensions in the movement about the life of our places, about affordability, about sustainability and the environment, and about financing and regional economics tell us that this is the case.

Chris Alexander, in describing the necessity for open source, generative processes that embody life, seems to be setting an impossible task. He is really reminding us of the inherent and creative tension within our movement. It's the tension between being true to our calling and making a living.

We are a set of visionary reformers who, at the end of each day, have to make it work in the world as it is, and Alexander reminds us that better isn't good enough, for the problems and pathologies we are trying to solve are deeply rooted in a set of processes that must be comprehensively transformed.

Almost 30 years ago, Christopher Alexander opened a set of doors and challenged architects and urbanists to walk through them. In this century, with *The Nature of Order*, he has opened a further set of doors and issued a next challenge. It is for that reason that, on behalf of the Congress for the New Urbanism, I am proud to present Christopher Alexander with one of the two inaugural Athena Medals.

Part 7.
Urbanism in Late-Stage Capitalism

Big seems to get bigger, and the bigger things get, whether they are projects, buildings or corporations, the crappier they seem to become.

In developed economies, housing has ceased to be shelter and become investment, and land and buildings have become commodified. And yet, people's needs for shelter, for work, for exchange and celebration have not changed.

These articles explore means of ensuring that those needs are met in a time when the prime directive seems to be delivering a 30 percent return to the shareholder.

Part 2

Urbanism in Late-Stage Capitalism

Post-Truth Architecture in the Age of Trump

Building Design

March 7, 2017

Donald Trump is the first developer to become president, and his proposal for a Mexican border wall shows he knows a lot about the usefulness of architecture in marketing and symbolism. Architecture has often been a political football.

The intrinsic qualities of commodity, firmness and delight have long been agreed the essentials of architecture, though in these relativist days, delight has come in for a bit of a kicking. How architecture conveys status, wealth, or class has been the subject of more debate, but it is undeniable that both architects and their clients have sought to tell a story about themselves through their buildings.

The intended messages have varied over time, yet the use of the act of building to signify has not. Nor has the identification of architecture with a particular time ceased to be used as a cudgel in the style wars. The architects of the Enlightenment saw classicism as representing logic, rationality and a brighter future. The framers of the United States constitution saw the architecture of the Greeks as symbolic of democracy and freedom from despotism. Ruskin and Pugin argued that classicism was pagan, idolatrous and enslaving, elevating the Gothic style as the embodiment of piety and honesty. Later generations have picked up this theme, associating classicism with fascism and slavery.

Modernism has undergone the same transitions and appropriations. Beginning with the Bauhaus ideas of craft and simplicity, modernist architecture was soon saddled with erasing class barriers, creating housing for all and ushering in the freedoms of the machine age. With the International Style, modernism became the symbol of globalisation, and in recent years, high tech architecture has strayed far from its socialist roots to become the mode of expression for corporations and high-net-worth towers.

Of course the association of a particular style with a particular ideology is nutty, but architecture does establish hierarchy and the more important buildings do tell us what an epoch values—whether it is cathedrals, palaces, parliaments, or shopping malls and luxury tower blocks.

And in the post-truth world it seems one doesn't even have to build the building to brandish it as totem. The announcement that Paris will build seven new towers in La Defense as home for the capital and companies that will flee a post-Brexit Britain has already served its purpose, whether or not the buildings are actually constructed, by sending a signal that even as Britain closes its doors, France and Europe are opening them for investors.

Even when a building is built, it can be post-factual. The Trump Organization opened a new Trump Tower in Vancouver this month, touting it as the first new tower in six years and as Vancouver's largest building of 69 storeys. In fact, it is Vancouver's second tallest building, numerous buildings have opened in recent years and it is only 62 storeys high. This kind of size inflation is not new to Donald Trump, Trump Tower in New York is claimed to be ten storeys higher than it really is. Trump has repeated this trick at least seven other times.

The biggest symbol of Trump's Presidential campaign was the border wall with Mexico. Borrowing imagery from Cold War Berlin, he has promised to build the "biggest, beautifulest wall" to keep all "the bad hombres" in Mexico out. Campaign promises that Mexico will fund the wall have unravelled and a recent report found that of the more than $21 billion US needed to build the wall, only $20 million is available—not enough to even begin construction. Nevertheless, the Trump Administration has begun soliciting architects and engineers.

My modest proposal for this alternative-fact universe is that Trump's team only commission a model and fly-through video of the wall, as that would likely satisfy both The President and his supporters. It could be shown at rallies and on cable TV. If this approach is successful, I would like to extend the idea to many contemporary building proposals. Perhaps a new prize could be established for the best post truth building, saving the rest of us from its reality?

Finally, Some Smart Thinking About Garden Cities

Building Design

September 9, 2014

The announcement of the winner of the £250,000 Wolfson Prize on Garden Cities last week mostly was framed as another attack on the green belt.

Ballyhooed as the second largest economics prize after the Nobel, its 2014 focus on Garden Cities made it the rival of the Pritzker and Driehaus in architecture. Unlike all of these awards, though, the Garden City Wolfson Prize was a contest, not a recognition of career accomplishment and it attracted a wide range of aspirants.

A review of the five finalists—Barton Willmore, Shelter, David Rudin with Nicholas Falk from Urbed, Chris Blundell, and Wei Yang and Partners—reveals the depth of thought and work that went into the entries. The entrants have exposed many of the challenges that underpin trying to deliver more and better housing.

Interestingly, none of the finalists argue for less planning. Rather, they argue for better planning and for doing a better job of developing agreements with local communities about new growth. There was a divide between top-down and bottom-up approaches, with Barton Willmore calling for a Royal Commission to pick the new town sites and national legislation updating the New Towns Act. Shelter picked a single site in the Medway, while Chris Blundell identified a site near Maidstone and Wei Yang argued for an arc of garden cities between Cambridge and Oxford.

In the end, though, one can see why the Urbed entry won the competition. Drawing on their long practical and research experience, the authors unerringly point out the key problems with both the house builder business model and with NIMByism and propose bold though difficult solutions to both problems. They point out that reliance on brownfield land will only deliver about 60 percent of Britain's housing need and argue that their proposal can make up the difference.

Because house builders make their profit from uplift in land value, and because the market is dominated by a few large firms, Rudin and Falk argue there is no incentive for them to compete for quality or produce more homes. Rather, every incentive is for them to increase their margins. They argue that Garden Cities must acquire the land at or near agricultural value, building at the plot level and leaving putative uplift for the production of infrastructure such as schools, parks and reserves, and transport, energy and utilities. Their viability work confirms the feasibility of the approach. Many of the other approaches rely upon the mythical patient investor, willing to take a lower return for greater profits over time.

Second, they note that UK urban extension policy has focused on adding at the edges of towns and cities in a way that connects and that this invariably arouses next-door neighbours. Instead they propose satellite extensions connected with tram lines, each of sufficient size to be considered a town and possessing town infrastructure but connected to an existing city. In form, they are more like Australia's garden city of Canberra, which after 100 years is belatedly getting its tram network. By placing these satellites in what the authors call undistinguished green belt away from neighbours, they hope to be able to develop a Compact with residents of the existing city on benefits and protections for them.

I think the Urbed team is right that new Garden Cities must emerge as extensions to existing cities, for they need to rely upon mainline transport infrastructure and cultural, business and educational entities to succeed, else they will be merely outsized suburbs.

I am somewhat less convinced that the political will can be found to take green belt land from agricultural use, either at the local or national level. It will depend upon skilled engagement strategies, the building up of trust and some kind of guarantee that the same old housing estates won't in the end be built. Urbed proposes to rely less on volume builders and more on self build, private rented stock and the like, and to take the time to do it well. But this will be resisted as well.

In the end, the Wolfson Prize provided a real service in bringing such a level of analysis and thought to the question of meeting housing demand, and it should provoke ongoing dialogue, education, and follow through, both nationally and locally.

Garden Towns Need Some Garden City Thinking to Succeed

Building Design

January 4, 2017

Much effort has been expended by successive governments in stimulating production by volume house builders, with modest success. Some estimate that planning permission has been granted for over 600,000 homes, though the number of actual housing starts, while up, hovers stubbornly around the 2008 figure. New Labour tried to change this by various stratagems: 'modern methods of production,' aimed at stimulating competition by introducing new entrants, and 'eco towns', new settlements bearing a green label. In the end both came to naught.

Over the past few years the new settlement idea has been taken up by the Conservative government, under the banner of garden towns and villages. It is as important to understand what these so-called garden settlements are. These are intended to be stand-alone communities, with villages having between 1000–10,000 units and associated local services and garden towns comprising more than 10,000 houses and services. They are locally sponsored, with 14 garden villages and 3 garden towns announced at the beginning of this week after a competition. Seven garden towns have already been announced.

These garden towns and villages are not, except insofar as they are new settlements, the heirs to Ebenezer Howard's garden cities, which were meant to be financed by capturing the "unearned increment," or the uplift in land value from obtaining planning permission, for the provision of needed infrastructure and services. Garden towns were meant to be satellites of a central city, and had clear planning and design theories associated with them. In contrast, the Government's new policy clearly states that there is no planning or design theory associated with garden towns and villages, and is silent on the relationship between the towns and the nearby city. This is in contrast to Urbed's Wolfson prize paper, which postulated a clear linkage, both with transport and economy, to a nearby central city.

A cursory review of the entries reveals a mixed bag, ranging from sites under multiple ownership to sites controlled by a single landowner and from sites which are closely linked to nearby cities to stand-alone sites in areas of low housing demand. Some have the opportunity for jobs, others will do well to attract a local shop and a primary school. All are eligible for various government subsidies, including the Starter Homes programme, and all are to be granted various "planning freedoms" and are urged to have "quality designs."

Just before Christmas, The Prince's Foundation issued a report which bears upon this issue of quality and the provision of services. The report, entitled "Building a Legacy," argues that landowners should take a more prominent role in taking sites through the planning process, and that doing so will not only improve quality but benefit them financially. Focusing on developments at a scale similar to those proposed in the garden towns and villages programme, the report argues that providing infrastructure, needed amenities and design quality is feasible under the landowner model in areas where sales prices exceed £250/sq. ft. and where the build out will take more than seven years. The report provides a number of case studies, most sponsored by landed estates which have often tended to take a longer-term view of value.

The jury is out whether there are sufficient numbers of individual landowners with both the vision and the resources to take these kind of large-scale projects forward, but the legacy model described by The Prince's Foundation applied equally to potential settlements on public land. Indeed this was the model formerly applied by English Partnerships, one of taking the site through master planning, garnering an outline permission on the whole site, providing road and utility infrastructure and then selling each phase pursuant to a design code.

Whether private landowner, public land, or multiple landowners, the key to achieving quality is to accompany the master planning and public engagement process with either an outline planning permission, a local development order or Supplemental Planning Guidance covering the whole new settlement. One could even take the precedent of the New Towns to heart and acquire the land through compulsory purchase prior to planning and apply Howard's dictum of utilising the uplift to provide infrastructure and services.

The Government is to be commended for putting the idea of new settlements on the table again. But if this programme is to succeed in producing something other than very large-scale housing estates, government policy should be more explicit in requiring and providing the resources for master planning and design guidance for the entire settlement, accompanied by some form of planning permission, as well as a mechanism for value capture to fund all the elements of a town. It wouldn't hurt to require all the winning proposers to read Ebenezer Howard's *Garden Cities of Tomorrow*, either.

Here's the Detail That's Missing from All the Manifestos

Building Design

May 13, 2017

It is election season and all of the party manifestos are worried about the housing crisis.

Labour promises to build a million homes and 100,000 council or housing association homes a year, without resorting to "rabbit hutches." The Conservatives also want to build a million homes, and wish to increase council and housing association numbers, with an emphasis on matching "the quality of those we have inherited from prior generations." They aim to do this by building more "mansion blocks, mews houses and terraced streets." The Liberal Democrats promise to build 300,000 homes a year, including direct building by councils. They will create a bank and build 10 garden cities. The Green Party manifesto calls for 100,000 social rented homes a year and for tripling a land value tax.

Despite the welcome focus on housing, the manifestos devote little but rhetoric to the question of ensuring that these large numbers of new homes enhance the quality of people's lives and the quality of the cities, towns and villages in which they are built.

Market towns and smaller cities across the country are already seeing the impact of massive urban extensions built out by volume house builders with standard house types, urban plans and "optimised" supply chains. And the residential tower built for investors that has become ubiquitous in London is creeping into other cities as well.

Incoming RIBA president Ben Derbyshire wants to have a housing expo on a grand scale to showcase architect-led housing. Last year's Starter Homes initiative proposed a return to the pattern books favoured by Georgian and Victorian builders. And Create Streets' Nicholas Boys Smith has called for a "direct planning revolution," tying the use of permission in principle and local development orders to form-based design codes.

It might be worth parsing how and where these three solutions work best to improve design quality, for they each have different applications, and all should be in the toolkit.

It is unlikely that most PLC builders will suddenly change their spots and commission architects to design housing schemes, although landowner-led projects such as the Duchy of Cornwall's Newquay and the Chapelton of Elsick in Scotland do tend to be led by architects. Most housing is presently built by the volume builders using in-house plans and types.

The architect-led approach can have a real impact in the building of new council homes and perhaps with the more enlightened housing associations. There is a long and bright history of high design quality in council housing, and it is here that the design expo could make its sale. Architects can also play a leadership role in smaller schemes, such as cohousing, custom and self-build. With large sites, it will be important to employ multiple architects to ensure variety.

Pattern books were the tool of choice for builders in Victorian and Edwardian times, as a clear and graphic way of communicating a shared grammar and vocabulary about building. They work best when they accompany a strategic masterplan, and when a master developer wants to direct to multiple builders working across a larger site.

Form-based design codes are not a new idea, as they were employed with great success in Edinburgh's New Town. Americans have promoted them as an alternative to the rigid functional zoning that produced cookie cutter suburbs across the United States, and there was a flurry of interest in them in the 2000s, when English partnerships employed design codes on a number of large schemes. Architects tended to view coding with suspicion, as a brake on their creativity, and house builders tended not to like them because they forced them to vary from their standardised templates and supply chains.

The concern of architects may be overblown, as most large housing schemes don't use multiple architects anyway, and design codes are a way of ensuring that multiple architects are employed. Most people remember the new urban town of Seaside from its stage dressing for the Truman Show, but its design code sought to create a harmonious streetscape and encourage quality, while providing guidance to the huge number of architects who built individual homes or flats there. These included architects as diverse as Deborah Berke and Rural Studio's Sam Mockbee, Leon Krier and Machado and Silvetti, and Aldo Rossi and former Yale dean Robert AM Stern.

Design codes work best as a tool of the planning system, while pattern books are a developer's tool. Design codes make sense when a local authority, neighbourhood forum or landowner wishes to ensure urban and architectural quality—variety within a pattern—over a geographic area with multiple landowners and/or multiple builders.

The code can be linked to tools in the planning system, including permission in principle, and local and neighbourhood development orders, to provide an expedited path for developers and builders. A neighbourhood plan which identifies a number of small sites in a neighbourhood or village could, for example, include a neighbourhood development order granting permitted development rights so long as the design code was employed. Similarly, a local authority wishing to encourage self or custom building could devise a new plotland model, selling serviced plots with permission in principle pursuant to a design code.

These approaches restrict the freedom to create of the developer, the house builder or the architect in the public interest. Putting architects as the head of the team restricts the use of standard models. Pattern books tend to be style based. Design codes tend to define massing, allowable building types, street orientation and other elements of urban form, but need not be style based.

Both design coding and pattern books can be outgrowths of a user-driven process, and schemes led by architects can use a charrette model to better reflect user and resident concerns. These approaches can in turn help to address concerns over development, which by and large have to do with the impact of new development on quality of life.

Letter to Edward Glaeser in Response to "Two Green Visions: the Prince and the Mayor," in *Triumph of the City*

January 2011

Dear Professor Glaeser,

First of all, kudos to you for your book *Triumph of the City*, but also for your ongoing critical thinking and research into urban and metropolitan issues and the economy. I have been inspired, challenged and educated by your work for some years now, and as a planner and policy person, found myself signing onto NBER years ago largely to have access to your papers.

I am writing to correct various points made by you in your chapter on the work of the Prince of Wales in building and the environment, which in my view have missed the point about His Royal Highness's work in this field. Poundbury was conceived as a radical antidote to the urban sprawl prevalent in both the UK and US since World War II, and remains unique in its commitment to put shops, schools and workplaces amongst homes. This rich mix creates the possibility, if not the absolute rule, that people might walk to these amenities rather than take their cars. If cars remain a popular modal choice in Poundbury, and the residents prefer small- and medium-sized row houses over flats (there are, in fact, no large houses in Poundbury comparable to those in the US) this reflects the fact that the development is not an autocratic realm based on dictate but an immensely popular, market-facing, commercial development. In this, the Prince, through the Duchy of Cornwall, is acting as an environmentalist of persuasion, changing the habits of many rather than passionately preaching to an already converted few.

Something like 30 percent of the current home-building at Poundbury is, in fact, apartments—in line with current UK planning guidance. Whilst the surrounding countryside is attractive, Poundbury is also emphatically an urban place, representing the main extension to the county town of Dorchester, with easy, walkable access to its amenities and job opportunities. It is also twice as dense as surrounding neighborhoods and its town center is presently being built out with high-density, mid-rise buildings. In this, Poundbury is as much a part of twenty-first-century Britain's lifestyle as the sort of high-rise apartment promoted by Ken Livingstone as mayor of London. It is a question of building at scales appropriate to the context—and Poundbury is an extension to Dorchester, a market town in Dorset, not a neighborhood in London, Edinburgh or New York City.

You may be interested to learn that the Prince's Foundation for the Built Environment, of which HRH is President, advocates, like you, for transit-oriented development, denser agglomerations of apartments in city locations, as well as streets, squares and public spaces designed around people's needs rather than those of the car.

We entirely share your view that "In cities…people end up sharing common public spaces, like restaurants, bars and museums." This is good for the environment, and is reflected in our mixed-use, urban plans, the practical outcome of our advocacy of car-free city living. I have myself published both research and opinion arguing for density and design as critical factors in city success, both environmentally and economically.

I only take issue with your assumption that this vision of modern urban life is necessarily high-rise in every location, or styled á la Richard Rogers. Rudimentary environmental science now argues against the relevance of the steel frame and the glazed wall to a "green" building vocabulary—our prototype low-carbon home designed for the UK Building Research Establishment achieves energy efficiency with solid-wall thermal mass.

Moreover, as we have learned from our outreach and our own observations, the most appealing images of city life for aspirant home buyers are not Canary Wharf or Roger's austere towers but mid-rise, dense, human scaled communities such as Greenwich Village or

Tribeca in NY, and Bloomsbury or Kensington in London. Interestingly enough, the densest London borough is the Royal Borough of Kensington and Chelsea, predominantly built out with terraces of three stories (rowhouses in American parlance) and five to seven story mansion blocks of flats with shared garden courtyards. These are also, incidentally, the places people vote for time and again with their wallets, making them amongst the highest value real estate in the world.

We had the chance to apply some of this thinking in a project we undertook in Walthamstow, a diverse outer London town center, with support from the London Development Agency and the Mayor's office, when Ken Livingstone was mayor.

There we sought to dramatically increase density in a very transit accessible location in the face of determined neighborhood opposition to the proliferation of developer towers fitted out with two-bedroom flats. We were able to replan the entire town center with infill of mid-rise buildings, and to demonstrate that we could achieve higher densities in this way than with tower-block buildings. The plan was overwhelmingly supported by the public and adopted after extensive consultation by the local authority. This case is documented in my 2008 book *Transport and Neighbourhoods*.

So I feel we are not wildly divergent in environmental theory but differ in our stress on mid-rise density rather than high-rise density, and proportion and thermal mass in buildings to make them long lasting and durable, rather than a reliance on technological add-ons. As Prince Charles said at our annual meeting in 2008, "Many people believe, erroneously, that the only way to achieve environmental efficiencies in development is by building very tall buildings." Indeed, improving the average density of building in England is critical to achieving "location efficiency," which reduces automobile use and greenhouse gas emissions, as well as minimizing land-take. But these efficiencies only begin to occur at 17 units to the hectare, when public transport becomes feasible, and begin to tail off at densities above 70 units to the hectare, according to a definitive research study from the United States which has recently been applied by The Prince's Foundation in a London project. This is because achieving environmental gains is a function of density, access to public transport and walkable, connected streets.

"If clustered, then the virtue of height becomes something that can, in the hands of creative architects, be truly celebrated. This solution, so clearly the case in Manhattan or La Défense in Paris, requires locations where intrusion into historically protected views, either at height or at street level, can be avoided, and is, therefore, difficult to justify in places such as the City of London where the pressure to build at height is often greatest." HRH The Prince of Wales, "New Buildings in Old Places," January 31, 2008.

I look forward to meeting you in person at some point, and discussing this issue further. I appreciate that the contrast between Prince Charles and Red Ken makes for a good story, but I think we are allies, and hope we can find common ground. I understand that you will be speaking at the Congress for the New Urbanism meeting in Madison, Wisconsin in early June. I will also be at that event, and perhaps we could find time for a chat when you are there.

Warm regards,
Hank

Can Smart Urban Design Tackle the Rise of Nationalism?

Building Design

July 5, 2016

On the centenary of Jane Jacobs' birth, architects and planners lauded her book *The Death and Life of Great American Cities*. Both loved and reviled upon its release, it has come to be seen as one of the essential books about the city and the importance of lively, diverse neighbourhoods, the housing stock and a more incremental approach to building the city. Her nickname, St Jane, obscures the fact that she was a famously tough activist who waged battle with the planning and design professions for most of her life, who belittled her as a housewife. Today she is seen as a key exponent of a more organic approach to planning and design.

Jane's work on the economy of cities occupied her for much of the rest of her life. And here too she was generally rubbished by the economists for her lack of formal education. But her book *The Economy of Cities* opened up a needed examination of the urban scale just as it was becoming clear that metropolitan regions do compete as entities in the global economy, and her idea of promoting a sustainable economy based on locally sourced labour and resources is one that smart city economic development officers have embraced.

Jane Jacobs' last book was *Dark Age Ahead* in 2004 and the New York Times review called it an "extremely sloppy book" with a "lack of methodology," and other reviewers were also unconvinced that the western way of life was teetering on a precipice. After *Creative Class* author Richard Florida commended its prescience recently, I decided to have another look at its argument.

Perhaps in 2004 it was difficult for many to see disaster on the horizon, as the American Empire was in its post-Iraq triumphalist stage, and the economy has not yet begun its 2008 faltering. Yet Jacobs identified a number of long-term trends that should have caused some disquiet at the time: the decline of family/community support structures in the face of modernity and urban restructuring and migration, the failure of professions and trades such as accounting and manufacturing to police themselves through guilds and professional associations, rampant consumer culture, a lack of respect for science and bad science, and the evolution of higher education from learning to what she called credentialing to guarantee higher salaries.

These diverse pathologies had in common a dislocation from both people and place, underpinned by bigness and the rise of the corporation as a super citizen, endowed with both human and extraordinary rights and privileges. Jacobs looked back at other dark ages and characterised them as a time of forgetting of both knowledge and values, and noted that those areas which prompted recovery from past dark ages had preserved knowledge in monasteries, universities or in trades.

The rise of Donald Trump in the United States, Nigel Farage here and nativist parties across Europe, combined with the pre-modern rantings of the Islamic State, certainly seem to indicate amnesia about the values that have animated us since the Second World War: respect for human rights and for providing opportunity for all, a belief in the benefit of talking together as one world, and a collateral belief in the rule of law. Resurgent nationalism and tribalism take us back to a different time, of tough-talking strong men and nation states.

Underlying this forgetting is a disquiet among the populace who see the broader trends that Jacobs spoke of so often as leaving them out, and it is that failure to define a future for the post-industrial cities and towns of the developed world and the rural parts of the global south that causes dislocation from culture and tradition and generates anger and extremism.

When Jane Jacobs talked about the failure of the family she was really talking about the family as a part of the structure of villages, towns and neighbourhoods, and not as the nuclear family relocated to the suburb or to the housing estate. Jacobs called *Dark Age Ahead* a hopeful book, and as always she saw the hope in urbanism, in lively diverse organic neighbourhoods in cities with mixed economies.

In the dozen years since the publication of her book recognition has come of the role of cities in sustainable development, in creating a civic culture and in improving education and the status of women, with the UN adoption of the Sustainable Development Goals and the forthcoming New Urban Agenda at Habitat 3 in Quito this October. As laudable as these developments are, they point to the fundamental misfit between the nation state and the global economy, in an era when metropolitan regions are core actors.

The desire for nationalism evidenced in Brexit is a shrinking away from meeting the real challenges ahead. While it is understandable to recoil from dark forces, modernity is not going away and the economically and culturally diverse metropolitan regions and city/town are the vehicles for embracing modernity. As architects and planners it is incumbent upon us to try to reconcile this conflict by defining a modernity that embraces and reinforces local culture and tradition while meeting contemporary needs.

If the characteristic of the Dark Age is forgetting, then it is the collective memory embodied in the cities and towns we design for and are stewards of that may preserve the values to help us deal with the unwritten future.

2011 Founders Forum on the New Urbanism at Seaside, Florida

Contribution to an Unpublished Book

I had to be dragged kicking and screaming to my first Congress for the New Urbanism. It was Congress III in San Francisco, and Peter Calthorpe was reaching out beyond the first group of founders to housing, environmental and transportation activists. Hooper Brooks of the Surdna Foundation and Hal Harvey of the Energy Foundation, who were both funders of the Surface Transportation Project where I was executive director, more or less insisted that I go. Even that early on, there was street talk about the New Urbanism, and I didn't like what I was hearing. Elitism, top-down, designer-focused: all of it added up to something very different from the community-engagement model I was peddling as a campaigner against roads and the highway lobby.

The fact, that it was in San Francisco helped, as it was a town I knew well, having lived there and in LA for most of my life. And I admired Peter Calthorpe's pedestrian-pocket ideas and his work with Sim Van Der Ryn and Jerry Brown. But what I found when I got to the Sheraton Palace Hotel altered the course of my life. First of all, as Shelley Poticha—then of Calthorpe's office—checked me in, I discovered she was married to one of my oldest friends from university days. And that certainly broke the ice.

We were herded into the ballroom and took part in an endless plenary composed of the newbies whom Peter had assembled for the Congress. From memory, it included people like Stewart Brand, Neal Pierce, John Parr, and Bob Yaro. I began my talk with a cheap shot about meeting in a posh hotel, and the barriers it raised to outreach, and Peter has, quite properly, never let me forget it.

CNU III was about the regional scale, and as a regional and transport planner, I was thrilled. I was delighted to see people like transportation reformer Walter Kulash there, and by the end of the Congress,

I was beginning to want to be part of this new thing. The energy, the ideas, and above all the practical commitment to dealing with the guts of the sprawl machine and trying to fashion places worth living in all attracted me. I was reassured as well by the clear commitment to social change that underpinned the work of the founders.

At the Surface Transportation Policy Project we were working with Senators Moynihan and Chafee and Congressman Mineta to alter national policy to favor transit-oriented, walkable metropolitan regions and reduce the cars- and highways-only nature of the transport planning and funding system in the country. We were also beginning to talk with the National Trust, the 1000 Friends groups, NRDC, and the American Farmland Trust about creating Smart Growth America. The idea that the Congress for the New Urbanism could be the design/implementation partner to all of this policy work was an attractive one.

STPP and CNU began to publish case studies and two-page design briefs on street design and transit-oriented development, and we began to talk with the Institute of Transportation Engineers about guidance.

This work brought me back to planning and design, and reinforced my growing conviction that policy work, important as it may be, was not where I wanted to spend all of my time. All too often, I was seeing good policy turned into legislation or regulation and then ignored or circumvented by entrenched professional bureaucracies. At the same time, I rediscovered community engagement in urban design, the subject of my master's thesis and early working life.

All that led me gradually to investing my energy and time into the CNU, as a task force member, board member, and chair for five years, and eventually to a new life in England and The Prince's Foundation, where I have now been for six years.

The CNU: It's Broke, Don't Fix It
As a board member, it became clear to me that the Congress for the New Urbanism was formed around a cogent set of principles about community that were clearly shared and embraced by all. Those ideas have been brilliantly and fluently codified in the Charter for the New

Urbanism, ratified in Charleston, of which I am pleased to have been an original signer. Having tried to extend it on several occasions, I am convinced that the Charter both then and now embraces the extent of the agreement within the organization. Both attempts to amend it to incorporate advances in practice and theory such as the Transect and coding, and a somewhat successful but divisive attempt to adopt a codicil called the Canons to embrace a more holistic approach to nature and the environment ultimately failed to take the organization forward. In my mind at least, the Charter embraces the fundamental beliefs as well as the inherent tensions in the New Urbanism, both as an organization and as a movement.

The tensions express themselves as fundamental disagreements about where to place the New Urbanism on a number of axes. First, there is the core divide between master planning and organic evolution. Secondly, there is the divide between the market and the state. And finally, there is the human/nature question. I will try to describe each of these continuing conundrums in turn, and explain why I think it is counterproductive for the New Urbanism as a whole to try to resolve these ongoing disagreements.

Master Planning vs. Organic Planning
Within the Prince's Foundation, we describe the debate about master planning and organic evolution as the Krier/Alexander debate, meaning Leon Krier and Christopher Alexander. And we cherish both as mentors and founding fathers. For me, it enshrined the idea that in a contemporary era of large numbers, the task of the urbanist is to embrace enough of the skills and tricks of the top-down master planner to ensure form and quality, along with a stepwise, sequential approach that emulates an organic evolution as the project is built out.

For the most part, that means not being afraid to be specific about core aspects of design, while allowing scope for designers and communities that come after to react to contemporary circumstances. In a few projects, we believe we have developed such organic codes.

The various new urbanist listserves continue to proliferate this debate between master planning and generative urbanism, and diehard adherents of each approach continue to die hard. New members join, discover this debate and fire it up on an ongoing basis. But to me, it is one of those perennials that goes back to human nature, where the right answer is found in balance, in the maturity of the designer, and in evolving our technique. As a sort of philosophical Buddhist, I would argue for the middle path.

Regulation vs. the Market
The second split has been between those who argue that the New Urbanism needs only an unfettered market and an enlightened consumer to prosper, and those who believe that environmental and social policy and regulation are required to ensure fairness and reduce the dominance of monied interests that are fundamentally inimical to walkable mixed-use and mixed-income communities.

I hope that we are big enough to contain both ends of this ideological spectrum, which has at least two axes: the axis of individual liberty and state intervention, and the axis of the free market and the regulated market. (I doubt many in the New Urbanism are out and out socialists.) Indeed, over time, we have been able to incorporate both believers in school choice and proponents of state schools, transit supporters who argue for it from a market perspective, and those who defend it as a public utility, and believers in mixed-income housing through inclusionary zoning and subsidy and those who support it through deregulation.

Man vs. Nature
The third divide is the environment-vs-human debate. And I think this one is largely settled on an intellectual and practice scale by two things: the transect, which provides a tool for creating a balance at each scale of urbanism, and the evolution of what Tom Low calls "low impact" techniques, which allow the creation of good urbanism, habitat and responsible environmental practice, as a matter of course. We have learned a lot about achieving this balance by studying historic communities, and the ways that British towns and villages have accommodated nature, managed water, and husbanded and used local resources.

Where this debate has not been settled is at the level of dialectics.

As green has become the new black, the New Urbanism has stubbornly clung to its old argument that walkable urbanism is fundamentally more green than shiny high tech "green" object buildings, despite the fact that this argument has failed to break through for over a decade now. "The Canons" authored by Elizabeth Moule, Stefanos Polyzoides and myself with help from many others, was an attempt to resolve this impasse by imbedding walkable urbanism into a holistic framework of green planning and design that also included local sourcing and recycling, renewables, sustainable urban drainage and many other practices as core new urbanist ideas—which, in fact, they are as many of us have practiced them throughout our careers. The fact that it was so controversial showed me that many were still fighting the last war…

Andres Duany has correctly pointed to landscape urbanism as an attempt to capture the high green ground for object-oriented architecture, and has identified the adoption of environmental-sounding yet abstract terminology as the key challenge it poses for the New Urbanism. I think he is also right that the new urban lexicon needs to evolve and adopt an explicitly green vocabulary and grammar, reflecting the fact that our theory and practice has evolved to embrace sustainable techniques from agrarian urbanism to sustainable drainage to passive design.

Organization and the Movement: Messy Vitality
The New Urbanism is a movement, not just an organization. It was given birth by a group of founders who launched the Congress for the New Urbanism to build the movement, but the nonprofit never attempted to capture the whole of the movement. The charity I worked for considers itself a part of the movement, though we call ourselves traditional urbanists, sustainable urbanists and community capitalists, not new urbanists (the word doesn't travel that well to Great Britain, where the Romans, Saxons and Normans did some good urbanism). Along with INTBAU, CEU and the Canadian and Antipodean branches, The Prince's Foundation represents a vibrant extension of the core ideas around the world.

Inside the United States, New Urbanism is taken forward and

advanced by the Seaside Institute, the National Charrette Institute, Reconnecting America, the Center for Neighborhood Technology, The Project for Lean Urbanism, Strong Towns and the Local Government Commission, among many others. Partner groups in policy and in other sectors abound such as Smart Growth America, the NRDC, T4 America, and new urban interest groups inside professional bodies such as the American Planning Association and the Institute for Transportation Engineers. And despite all our moaning, New Urbanism is well represented in the academy.

New Urbanism is not the CNU, and this is a strength. And yet it remains a problem. As chair, I embraced what I called the messy vitality of the movement as a core strength, and defined the role of the CNU not as captain but as the big tent, and as an organization that should do two core things: service its members, and engage the professional and certifying bodies to change standards, policies and guidance that inhibit urbanism from being implemented on the ground.

In addition to these activities, it is logical that the main membership body should have an advocacy function, both with respect to national policy and in terms of public relations.

Where the CNU seems to have difficulty is in servicing both the broad rank of its members and in promoting the advancement of theory and practice. And by and large, the evolution of New Urban technique and thinking happens elsewhere: in allied organizations and through members in commercial practice or the academy. New developments are communicated through listserves, and only secondarily through the annual Congress, which now primarily serves the roles of generating income for the organization and providing a forum for the general membership.

The Congress doesn't really serve my needs as an international member of the CNU, as it primarily responds to the needs of its Unites States member base, and that base is profoundly uninterested in what is happening in the rest of the world. The sheer number of Congress sessions, there to promote the greater number of people, also undermines the ability to attend and be apprised of current leading practice.

This function used to be handled through the New Urban Councils, but there has not been one since the Green Council in 2007, initiated by John Massengale with The Prince's Foundation.

Where We Need to Improve
Such a joint forum might best be invitational, and could happen annually with a participant group about the size of the 100 people who came together at the Alexandria, Virginia Congress. The institution of such an event would be timely, as I think economic and political events internationally have created both crisis and opportunity for development generally and for urbanism in particular. The precipitating events/triggers are the following:

- The continuing economic downturn and the consequent rise in inequality;
- The impending increase in energy costs brought about by increased demand from the Global South and lesser availability of easily extractable fossil fuels;
- At least in the UK and Europe, the end of easy government funding, and lessened capabilities in the public sector;
- A complete breakdown in public confidence in government or business.

It is hard to predict the future, but it is certain that we aren't going back. The last decade has seen a complete revolution in information/communication technology, and the rise of the Chinese and Indian economies is likely to precipitate a further revolution as early adopters there leapfrog Western culture. The New Urbanism needs to take a step back, and prepare itself to take a similar quantum step forward, and this reinvention needs to happen now. It won't be managed by the CNU as an organization, as it principally is organized to service the broader membership and to advance its president's agenda of highway deconstruction. But the CNU will play a key role in cascading the new ideas to the broader membership.

There should be a reinvention: a comprehensive rethink and recasting, unshackled from the limitations of the Congress for the New

Urbanism as a nonprofit. There needs to be a redefinition of urbanism, from being principally a design issue, to undertaking the central questions of community, governance and finance, alongside the secondary questions of skills, delivery, management and maintenance.

It seems to me that we have to come up with both theory and practice that effectively addresses:

- **Techniques for engaging in the twenty-first century.** How do we engage community for real, at scale, using the best of available technology, blending expertise with local intelligence? What does a twenty-first century charrette look like? How does telecommunications enable broader engagement, and how does community engagement promote subsidiarity?
- **Financial and management delivery models.** It is clear that the existing financial models for development will continue to produce short lived, poorly built buildings and neighborhoods, and that regulation is not substitute for a commercial model that favors building for the long term. The problem is that long-term gains are not valued in an era where capital is mobile and the future is discounted, and so something has to give. We need to give over our attention to reinventing the practice of development, looking at the role of land in the equation, the need for supply chains for local and sustainable products, and ways to capture future value to enable present investment.
- **Communicating over the heads of the critics.** A few tired memes tend to dominate public understanding and press coverage of the New Urbanism: the coding of behavior a la "The Truman Show" and recent coverage about Celebration, the traditional vs modern line and people love their cars. At the same time, research consistently shows that people hunger for community, they just believe that it is impossible, and that there is no point aspiring to it. It is a shame that the CNU focuses its PR machine almost exclusively on highway battles, as there is a huge need for a sustained consumer outreach. The Prince's Foundation has attempted to put the bulk of our communications effort into engaging with the general public as opposed

to debating on their own terms with architects and planners in front of the general public.

The Foundation's 2008-2023 partnership with Britain's Ideal Home Show is a case in point, as it bypassed the traditional mediation by the press and communicates directly with people.

- **Do we need a theory?** Next, there is the question of engagement with the academy and under what terms we engage. There are two strands here: engaging on the basis of rhetoric, theory and practice (what I would call the air war) and engaging structurally with the provision of skills-based education (the ground war). With respect to the air war, many members put a good bit of work into this effort with appearances at academic conferences, the *Journal of Urbanism* and academic sessions at the CNU. The rap on the New Urbanism is that we are deficient in theory, despite lots of theory work by many friends in the academy. This will continue to be the story, as our leaders are practitioners, and our central methodology involves studying what works and improving on it (a deeply unsatisfying approach for the academy, although it is grounded in the same empiricism as science). I wish people good luck with this effort, but I am more interested in the ground war.
- **Built-environment education.** The idea of engaging structurally with skills-based built environment education means tackling head on the conclusion of the 1950 Oxford Conference on Architectural Education, which sought to change architecture from being a craft or a trade into a higher status profession taught in the great universities. This conscious shift, mirrored in planning with the move to defining planning as a social science, meant a de-emphasis on skills and an emphasis on theory. I am convinced this change in direction has been a disaster, and the increasing deification of people who produce abstractions and call them architecture proves the point. The ground war would thus involve redefining built environment education as a skill, learned through a combination of theory and practice, with the

theory being taught in a practical way through both hands-on work and the study of precedent. We are evolving such approaches to education at The Foundation and trying to extend them into a network of institutions, and I am pleased to see the emphasis on practical work in programs at Miami, Notre Dame, Andrews and Hampton. A long-term strategy is needed, and a working group to take forward a more practical, international approach to architectural and planning education is needed.

These challenges are only incidentally about master planning, or design coding, or about architecture. It's not that these areas don't need work, but it is that there are active and vibrant reinventions ongoing in all of these areas. Until we fundamentally take on the larger production systems—of capital, of professionals, of receptivity—we will continue tinkering delicately at the margins.

Stirring the Pot
In my unpublished Master's Thesis in the School of Architecture at the University of Texas, written under the influence of Christopher Alexander in 1980, I proposed a method of community-centered design grounded in *A Pattern Language*. In discussing the challenges of adopting such an approach I said that "Architects and planners almost certainly will not be receptive to the redefinition of their respective roles that is essential to this design method." Looking back at the history of the New Urban movement, I think I was guilty of understatement. The entrenched hostility of the establishment is due to the fundamental challenge the New Urbanism makes to their presumption of expertise.

In 1991, I was proud to be part of what we thought was a landmark effort to redefine US transportation policy in the post Interstate era, from highways only to a community-centered approach aimed at serving metro areas, accommodating transit, walking and cycling, and seeing transportation as a means to the end of more livable vibrant communities. Flushed with excitement after attending the bill signing, I attended a lunch with one of the bill's authors, Public Works Committee Chairman Norman Mineta. As the lunch broke up, he told me that it would take at least thirty years to turn things around. I think that Congressman Mineta, later to become Secretary Mineta, was also guilty of understatement.

We are engaged in a long-term, multigenerational campaign. And success will involve both perseverance and adaptability. I would argue that we should not be too bound by the structures that have served us in the past. They will be fine.

The opportunity exists to imagine some new framings of our collaborative work together, some new platforms from which to project, or to engage in the repurposing of existing platforms. I think it is time to stir the pot, lest the New Urbanism become content with become merely a boutique shop in the suburban mall that is global development.

Architects are Critical to Adapting our Cities to Climate Change

Building Design

September 6, 2016

This week saw two disparate events that nonetheless resonated for me. The first was the happy news that the world's two biggest emitters of carbon—China and the United States—had signed up to the Paris climate accords. And the second was the commemoration of the Great Fire of London during the seventeenth century, with the burning of a scale model of London.

While much of the focus in Paris was on mitigating carbon, through both renewable energy infrastructure, and more compact and connected urban form, there is increasing evidence that we may have to adjust to two degrees or three degrees of temperature rise in any event, from the carbon already in the atmosphere and accelerating impacts in the Arctic and the oceans this causes. Hence there is also an urgency to think about adaptation to increased storm events, higher temperatures, and coastal, riverine and surface level flooding and the damage all these cause to cities and buildings, as well as the disruption to services and infrastructure that accompany these disasters.

The Great Fire provides a useful lesson to human response to disaster. In the wake of the fire there was an initiative to build more fire-resistant cities along rational lines, with both Christopher Wren and Robert Hooke submitting rational, geometric urban plans in the place for the narrow, jettied London streets. As always seems the case, though, people rushed to rebuild on their plots. In the end, though, there was a positive result as the city that emerged was brick and stone, with parapets over the roof line, deeper window reveals and flat elevations—in short the Georgian style with us to this day. The limits of adaption are clear but it is possible.

Adaptive architectural responses have already emerged in the wake of events like Louisiana's Hurricane Katrina, the US East Coast's Hurricane Sandy and flooding in Gloucestershire and Cumbria. After Katrina, as people rebuilt in flooded areas in New Orleans and the Mississippi Coast, single order guidelines were adopted to raise the ground floor height to as much as six meters above ground, keeping interiors dry at the expense of urbanism and accessibility. Many of the costly and iconic houses architects designed for Brad Pitt's Make It Right had these features.

More considered responses have been to rebuild houses that can take a bath with robust materials, electrical and other services raised above flood level, and plans that allow goods to move upstairs more easily in a storm event. It is likely that future events will dictate further design responses, with changes in construction as a result.

At the same time, adaptation will have to address future planning in both existing communities and in new urban extensions. These will entail more careful siting and urban design, particularly in areas impacted by surface level flooding from adjacent development or farm land, and incorporating sustainable drainage in a way that integrates with the compact urban form needed for mitigation. Also needed will be changes in upland farming and grazing to allow more retention of rainwater, reducing the need for channelising rivers and then building elaborate flood defences to respond to this channelisation. It behooves us to study traditional communities here, including cities like Salisbury and Winchester with water meadows that have built in sustainable and resilient flood defense, which could be enhanced rather than encroached upon with development.

A third area for attention is the need to build redundancy and resilience into infrastructure, especially power and water services. One impact of these events is the loss of these services and disruption in the wider grid, and newer communities may have to be built with community-level renewable energy infrastructure designed to resist disaster events.

Finally, tough decisions will have to be taken in existing communities, especially on our coasts. As climate impacts worsen, we will see those with means migrating to safer locations and we can design and build adaptive and resilient communities for them. But our coastal towns have also become places of deprivation and resettlement from cities and these people are likely to see the impact. Improved defences, some relocation and rebuilding are all likely responses, and the retrenchment of government from social housing provision is likely to make addressing these issues more difficult.

For many years, climate policy experts didn't discuss adaptation to climate, for fear that it would distract from mitigating emissions. Now, however, we don't have the choice, and architecture and urban planning are going to be critical in building climate-resilient cities and towns.

You've Got to Hand it to Post-Modernism

Building Design

September 22, 2015

One of the more interesting events of this month is a series of tours sponsored by the National Trust of brutalist buildings across the country. In recent years the National Trust, under the last two directors general, has been determinedly shedding its fogeyish, country house image in favour of embracing increased turnover, talking about wider landscape, policy advocacy, modernism and now post-modernism. At the country houses, this has meant bigger car parks, concrete and steel visitor centres and cafes with wood cladding and gastropub food, and an increased emphasis on how people below stairs lived.

Of course, the membership of the National Trust is still overwhelmingly middle class and still mainly interested in the country houses, but as the baby boomers age, there is a growing audience for mid-century modern architecture, which is the architecture these people read about when they were young adults. The fad for brutalism fits right into this, and the Brutal Utopia tours beginning this week are a canny piece of marketing by the National Trust and its co-sponsors Urban Splash, the University of East Anglia and the Southbank Centre to its metropolitan audience, despite the fact that the National Trust doesn't own or operate any of these properties. In a less resource-constrained era, perhaps these events might have been promoted, with scholarship, by a refocused and energised Historic England.

While there are a few notable examples of private-sector brutalism, notably the Tricorn Centre in Portsmouth and Trinity Square in Gateshead, most brutalist buildings were publicly commissioned, and all of those on the tours are public-sector cultural or housing projects.

This makes the utopia part of the title relevant, as the South Bank, UEA and housing projects like Park Hill, the Barbican and Trellick Tower were expressions of confidence in the power of modern design ideas to change society for the better by ridding it of old notions like the street, the house, and the private garden and replacing them with walkways in the sky, flats and communal space. It was also an expression of an era where government was trusted to tackle social problems and expected to provide services, including education and culture, to the public.

Without getting into the old debate about the persistent desire of the British for the private house and garden, or the benefits of urbanism, it seems clear to me that much of the appeal of brutalism is a nostalgia for this optimism and vigour in the public sector, for we are so far away from that in today's world of austerity, privatisation and corporate provision of almost everything. And, indeed, the success of projects like the Barbican and the hopeful revival of Park Hill are due to their rescue in the market place—the Barbican as a middle-class enclave in the City, and Park Hill's rescue being due as much to the entrepreneurial energy of Urban Splash as to the government subsidies that have helped close the gap. Even the South Bank owes much of its recent success to its rebirth as a retail venue, a change that many felt had gone too far in recent proposals.

Nostalgia for activist governments that impose architectural theories upon the populace, particularly in social housing, is understandable among architects, but perhaps less so among the general public. For we (fortunately) don't live in a world where brutalist ideas of the city or of housing predominate, but in a world that was conquered by a movement reviled by architects: post-modernism. And the complexity of a post-modern world, dominated by marketing, diversity and disparity, leads back to a nostalgia for simpler times when government could be trusted to sort things out. The success of Jeremy Corbyn's Labour party insurgency may be another example of this desire to move away from the fractured corporate-dominated world we live in.

Ultimately, then, brutalism, at least within architecture, has to be seen as another part of a post-modern landscape: one that is unlikely to be reproduced and must be re-imagined with corporate sponsorship, consumer culture and middle-class aspiration to succeed. And so, like the classical revival and the National Trust's core business of country houses, brutalism ceases to be a utopian movement and becomes another consumer choice in a plural world.

Part 8: Lean Urbanism: Making Small Possible

Most jobs are created by small businesses growing slightly larger. Most of the places we love have grown up over time, with the work of many hands.

Yet today it seems like the deck is stacked against the small project. It shouldn't be eighty percent as hard to build four houses as it is to build four hundred, but that the way it feels.

These essays explore ways to advantage small and bring it to scale.

A Lean Urbanism for England: Making Small Possible and Localism Real

Leanurbanism.org, March 2015

Royal Assent for England's Localism Act in 2012 created a suite of rights and tools at the neighbourhood and community scale in England, including the community right to challenge and to build, neighbourhood planning and neighbourhood development orders. Localism was meant to bring planning and development decisions closer to the people, and create a positive framework for growth around engaged communities setting guidelines which protect local character and identity. In the two years since, localism has become something of a sacred cow. All three parties embrace it, but all three are conflicted.

Conservatives want to move away from central government control and so have advocated all of the community rights. They also want to be sure more house-building helps the economy to rebound, and so they have empowered inspectors to approve development applications and taken other planning and development decisions to the central government level.

The Liberal Democrats embrace the idea of localism, but they are worried about the pace of development and of the need for more housing, and so they are proposing centrally approved garden cities, just as the Labour government proposed eco towns.

Labour's embrace of localism has proved that they too are unclear on the concept of subsidiarity as they have proposed to make neighbourhood planning mandatory!

The implementation of localism reveals this continuing conflict between the ideal of delegation and empowerment and the habit of centralism and regulation, but it also reveals the real appetite for making small-scale development and community building easier.

Localism Is Tougher to Do Than to Promote
As attractive as the concept of localism is rhetorically, it is challenging to implement. Over 2000 neighbourhood plans are underway and 750 community assets have been registered, including 250 pubs and 150 parks and playing fields, and government has spent millions supporting groups like Locality and the Royal Town Planning Institute in helping get the processes off the ground.

Despite this activity, about two hundred forty plans have been adopted by referendum (no referenda have thus far failed to pass!) and only 65 local development orders adopted by a small number of local authorities. There is a general perception that localism hasn't worked. This is unfair, as there is huge interest, a lot of work underway and it does take time for plans to wind through the process, which has several stages.

However, the real issue is that localism has been treated not as a simpler, more responsive way to improve communities and promote enterprise and business activity, but as another layer of government. So while we have eliminated Area Action Plans, we have gained another layer of policy-driven neighbourhood plans, which very often fail entirely to come to grips with the actual physical and design choices that the neighbourhood will confront. Planning is not a design discipline in this country, so neighbourhood plans often become another confusing layer of jargon.

In designing the process with safeguards, such as approval by local authority, an inspection and a referendum, the result has been added complexity and time to the process. By funding process-driven organisations to help make it work, the government has compounded the process and reinforced the notion that there is little advantage for local authorities seeking to promote regeneration. This feeling is amplified by the perceived threat to councillors and officers from loss of control.

There have been a series of regulatory reviews undertaken, but the dominant voice in all of these—and small wonder, because they have the resources to engage with government—have been the large house builders, the larger developers, their membership associations and the professional associations. In the aftermath of a really necessary wave of simplification, we have seen the PLCs take the most advantage of the new flexibility, and often in challenging local authorities used to doing things the old way. Without practical support, rather than the kind of cheerleading support for civic activism proffered by Locality, small-scale local regeneration will lag behind, and planning reform will continue to be seen as the 'large developer's charter.'

There is a need to rely less on master plans and long term development strategies as the sole way to take things forward, as we have seen that complex master plans too often fail to make provision for changes in local or national circumstances—and the result is plans that do not get built, or if built, struggle. This trend away from the big scheme can be seen in the rise of the pop up, the "meanwhile" use and what's called tactical urbanism. These are all temporary interventions, while the large-scale development crawls through the approval process, or they represent the creativity of individuals who can't seem to get projects off the ground in a more durable way

Making Small Possible
What's needed—and what I hoped that the localism agenda would provide—is a middle scale between the pop-up and the visionary master plan. This middle scale might include pilot projects, incremental development projects as opposed to complex master plans, and efforts to empower individual property owners, custom builders, businesses and community organisations to improve their properties, put empty properties back into use, build new premises and work together to make community wide impacts through a number of linked but individual actions.

A "Lean" approach to building and revitalisation attacks the sclerosis that affects planning and review processes, with the goal of helping entrepreneurs, small business people and community groups with great ideas and without deep pockets contribute to their communities, put people to work and make nicer places. It would do this by slimming down codes and plans, challenging thresholds for regulation and finding workarounds and patches to the glitches, snags and snafus that seem to plague small and innovative projects more than they do the mundane lowest common denominator. A lean urbanism would be open-ended, allowing for incremental change, open access, reducing the barriers for ordinary people to extend their home, improve their business or develop community assets, and it would be open-source, providing tools and platforms that all can build upon.

The new community rights—right to bid, right to build and neighbourhood planning—and new flexibility for permitted development provide a strong platform for this kind of incremental revitalisation. And yet the perfect can be the enemy of the good, with rules and regulations often making small development unaffordable. A leaner urbanism would work on infill and suburban repair, at the scale of the building or the street, developing code-light zones, pilot projects, and building types which fit underneath thresholds for lifts or expensive kit.

The great divide in urbanism has always been between those who espouse the grand project—like Ebenezer Howard, Daniel "make no small plans" Burnham, Baron Haussmann and Le Corbusier—and those who celebrate the messy organic approach, exemplified by Jane Jacobs, Christopher Alexander and the community architecture movement in Britain.

Certainly, doing some things big is essential. But it does mean that the pace of change can be too fast for local communities, and the institutions which can take on large-scale change don't tend to be community or individually owned.

Community rights may thus be not only a tool for a leaner and more cost-effective scale of revitalisation, but also for one which is aimed at ensuring community benefit and control of the process—allowing revitalisation through investment in the social capital of a community as well as the built capital.

What's more, the gradual approach and sensitive knitting-together often seems to be what people want. In many communities, we find that small, funky workspaces are fully occupied, yet we don't seem to focus on making more of them. These small business spaces are still the backbone of the economy.

Trinity Buoy Wharf and the Tea Building in London, Birmingham's Custard Factory and Jewellry Quarter, and Bristol's Tobacco Factory are all good examples of reoccupation of older buildings gradually leading to more ambitious projects and the creation of hubs for innovation and knowledge.

The regeneration of the seaside community of Folkestone as an artists quarter got it right by putting the icon in last, after the community building part. In each case it took an entrepreneur with drive, patience, some undervalued space and the will to pursue the projects incrementally. All of these projects are job-creators, and all are founded on a yeasty mix of small and medium enterprise and creative and cultural assets. There is a lot to learn from them, and perhaps a learning network needs to capture information from community entrepreneurs.

Lean Urbanism and Development
Similar issues with process, complexity and time frames abound throughout the developed world, and I have been working with a group of developers, charitable foundations, architects and urbanists in the United States on a "Project for Lean Urbanism," Coordinated by an advisory group including urbanist and new town designer Andres Duany, urbanist and retiring Dean of the University of Miami School of Architecture Elizabeth Plater Zyberk and myself, and funded by a growing group of philanthropies, the project seeks to develop tools for leaner planning and coding, more cost-effective and less complex infrastructure and building types and leaner finance and enterprise. Over the next three years it is proposed to develop white papers, case studies and tool kits and to undertake pilot projects in a number of US cities.

The first gathering was hosted in Detroit in October 2013 and a second in San Diego, with a three-day seminar in Buffalo in June 2014. The effort is funded by the Knight Foundation and the Kresge Foundation in the United States, and pilot projects are being sponsored by local governments and local business communities in Savannah, Saint Paul, Chattanooga and Lafayette.

At the core of the lean project is the idea of targeting small-scale and incremental interventions in existing cities and suburbs that can identify, unlock and leverage hidden or under-utilised assets — be they built assets like vacant buildings or land or transport capacity, financial assets like social capital or crowd sourcing, community assets like housing associations, knowledge clusters or artist quarters, or natural assets.

Lean Urbanism in the UK
A lean agenda for England might seek to develop a series of tools and case studies outlining ways that people have used permitted development rights, community rights and local and neighbourhood development orders to accelerate the process of bringing empty properties back into use, starting up business or reactivating moribund high streets. It might also explore ways that under-utilised public land could be used for custom building or community facilities or live-work space, or subdivided into smaller plots to be taken forward by smaller builders. There might also be an explanation of lean building types, lean infrastructure and lean finance, all of which might be about doing eighty percent of the job, at twenty or thirty percent of the cost and time.

Finally, a lean agenda would explore how to build incrementally through one or more pilot projects that explore ways to use existing authorities and policies in new ways and leverage community and natural assets in new ways.

The following activities could be taken forward by The Project for Lean Urbanism UK:

- White papers and case studies to lay the framework for a "lean toolkit" outlining opportunities to short circuit process afforded by the localism and regulatory reforms, and studies of successful incremental development undertaken by small business, small developers, community entrepreneurs and Business Improvement Districts.
- Lean Pilots in communities to identify and leverage hidden opportunities and assets. In each community a lean scan would be used to develop not only the project idea but also to build the implementation partnership and engage the community fully. Each project would identify a "pink zone" where red tape is

lessened using tools already provided through planning reform, such as the Local Development Order and community rights.

Pilot projects might include some of the following elements:

- Following up a neighbourhood plan and using the localism tools—neighbourhood development order, community right to build and permitted development rights—to assist a community seeking to retain control over, but enable smaller-scale development.
- Right to custom-build: work with a local authority to designate a site for custom-building, plan and code it with a lean code, and facilitate "plotland" development.
- Identify a "pink zone" in a regeneration area, where red tape is lessened, utilising all existing tools to lower barriers to entry for small-scale development. A key aspect would be finding ways to bring empty properties back into use in a cost-effective manner. Instead of meanwhile uses, permanent uses in meanwhile locations.
- Lean hub: explore using a community interest corporation as a facilitator of a hub for small business, live-work space, and creative industry, utilising existing buildings, and working to reduce barriers to reuse.

Enabling Small Is a Big Thing
Some might argue that enabling small is antithetical to the widespread change that we need to meet massive problems like concentrated poverty, neighbourhood decline and climate change mitigation and adaptation. But this presumes that making small possible won't scale up, and this seems to be a matter of creating local and national platforms that support a large number of incremental improvements.

Lean urbanism may thus be not only a tool for a simpler and more cost-effective scale of revitalization, but also for one which is aimed at ensuring community benefit and control of the process—allowing revitalisation through investment in the social capital of a community as well as the built capital.

The pilot projects can test this thesis at the local level, while at the same time building the toolkits and the frameworks for taking Lean Urbanism to scale as a means to revitalise communities from the bottom up, while still meeting broader planning goals.

Pink Zones to Lighten Planning Red Tape

Building Design

November 11, 2014

Every government tries to reform planning, and this government has tried harder than most to simplify it, eliminating thousands of pages of regulations, cutting out the regional layer and creating a new layer at the neighbourhood level. Yet, as of October, only 59% of all local authorities had managed to adopt local plans, and complex projects can take from six to 12 years to move from inception to grant of planning permission.

The complexity of planning, environmental regulation and Section 106 funding negotiations has created formidable barriers to entry in the market place. The market for housebuilding in particular has become increasingly concentrated, with close to 70% of all housing completions by firms which produce more than 500 units per annum, up from just over half in 1995.

Last Friday, the Centre for Policy Studies released a report calling for creation of "pink zones" (pink meaning lightened red tape) in which planning would be simplified through local agreement and coordination. The report *Pink Planning* suggests the creation of pink zones could lead to "more and better homes for people throughout the country."

The authors hope that pink zones could attract new institutional funding, and behave more like the great estates, which sought to build value through quality. They also propose to ensure that a greater portion of development fees can be used locally, through up-front agreement between the local authority and the community on standards to be upheld and benefits to accrue. All this requires targeted legislation, but not a new layer of planning reform.

The notion of the pink zone was adapted from the work of the Project for Lean Urbanism, a US and UK effort with which I am involved with the American town planner Andres Duany. Lean urbanism seeks to encourage small-scale development by reducing barriers to entry for small-scale developers, including immigrants, millennial generation architects and contractors and makers. The project targets existing authority and guidance, using hacks, work-arounds and thresholds to allow both simpler new-build and retrofit, and will test the model through pilot pink zone projects. Small entrepreneurial and incremental building and development should move from being a heroic exception, such as at George Ferguson's Tobacco Factory or Bennie Gray's Custard Factory, to being a natural step for a contractor or young architect to take.

The most powerful existing tool for simplifying planning is the Local Development Order (and its Neighbourhood corollary) allowing local authorities to give an upfront grant of planning permission to specified types of development within a defined area, with conditions to ensure quality. The Planning Advisory Service found in January that only 65 of these had been adopted, in a few councils and overwhelmingly for employment and not housing. The PAS found that both officers and members were reluctant to relinquish control and, in many areas, the LDO came with detailed conditions, requiring both later developer and authority effort.

Unless local authorities can resolve their reluctance to let go of control early in the process, simplified planning may have unintended consequences of adding layers of process. The Project for Lean Urbanism will address this through pilot projects, demonstrating success in some useful contexts such declining high streets in market towns of suburbs or in custom-build or small-scale housing zones. The Centre for Policy Studies proposes to create a powerful incentive for pink zones by dedicating fees to address local benefit and impact in pink zones.

Both ideas will have to deal with the challenging issue of assuring elected members and the public that reducing complexity can lead to improved quality of development. For most residents feel that new development generally makes their communities worse, based on their experience over the last 50 years—and proving the exception in advance is the real challenge. But the prize for encouraging small scale again might be that community architecture/development again becomes a career possibility for young architects and other built environment professionals.

Big Ideas Don't Often Produce Great Architecture

Building Design

June 15, 2012

Separating issues of urban design and architecture into neat political boxes is always a messy business. As a transplanted American, I find it doubly challenging, with ideas that I grew up viewing as left wing, here thought to be revanchist Tory notions, and vice versa.

Two of my columnist colleagues at BD have dared to enter this territory, challenging the left to promote a future urban vision. Wouter Vanstiphout decries the token nature of urban farms, and pop-up hipster shops while Owen Hatherley waxes nostalgic for the big imprints of post-war modernism. Both call for big new ideas to emerge, with the boldness of the neo-liberal alternatives at Canary Wharf or the big-brotherism of Park Hill and the Abercrombie plans. The implication seems to be that in an urbanising world we need big solutions, not "elective, hobbyist vanguards."

To me this bypasses the central problem: the fact that most urbanist theories of the modern era depend on either a Big State approach or a Big Corporate approach, and that's not how great cities are made. Neither Big State nor Big Corporate have produced great urbanism.

In the modern era, Big State generated the iconic cultural building and the isolated tower in the park, while Big Corporate treats buildings as commodities and reduces them to identikit, pedestrian low-rise estates, malls, business parks and the like.

Both will be on display at the Olympics, with Westfield centre the corporate solution, planning its big semi-public space squarely between the Olympic Park and the rest of the world. And in the Park and Village we will see the iconic object buildings in space and a big boxy housing estate of repeated buildings.

Wouter Vanstiphout is being rather hard on the poor hipsters and their markets and food halls. I see them as a creative response to the current economic situation and as an assertion of local identity. In our neighbourhood planning work we find similar tactical urban ideas emerging: in housing estates in Tottenham, East Lancs towns, community buildings in Toxteth, and leafy places like the South Hams and St Albans. Young hipsters don't have a monopoly on creative interventions.

I don't know whether Jane Jacobs-type approaches are left or right. But the ready assumption that just because we are dealing with large numbers we have to adopt a Fordist approach is dangerous, and the answer lies in parsing carefully between what the state does well—infrastructure, planning frameworks and enabling financial tools—and what entrepreneurial capitalism does well—bespoke solutions, efficient delivery and continuous improvement.

The drive toward localism by this government has created a number of tools for the third sector as well. Community right-to-build, self-build, neighbourhood plans and the like offer the opportunity to take some of the ideas being tried out by the Hoxton hipsters and the St Albans and East Lancs residents to scale. It may be my New World outlook, but I find much to cheer about among the myriad small interventions. To me they speak of empowerment, and that's a good thing.

Riding the Railroad to Revival

Building Design

May 8, 2015

A trip to the United States this month found the cities I visited—Miami, Dallas and Oklahoma City—in different stages of a building boom. I attended a meeting of smaller-scale developers sponsored by the Urban Land Institute in Miami and the annual gathering of more than 1,200 new urbanists in Dallas-Fort Worth. I found similarities and differences with Britain, both in the type of building going on and in the way it is affecting first-, second- and third-tier cities.

Like London, Miami seems to be a locus for foreign investment in residential property. Central Miami is seeing the construction of lots of new high-rise residential towers, similar in form and construction to those going up in London. There is one striking difference: the first six to 10 storeys of the towers are generally dedicated to parking because of the auto dependence of the city.

Towers underway include three "peanut"-shaped buildings by OMA, Zaha Hadid's 60-storey One Thousand Museum and, not to be undone, local firm Arquitectonica's 80-storey One Brickell City-Centre, which the Federal Aviation Administration has proposed to reduce in height by more than 50% to reduce conflict with overflying aircraft. As in London, there seems to be a fashion for trophy buildings by prominent architects but, unlike London, these buildings are concentrated largely in and near the city centre.

Sprawling Oklahoma City has the largest land mass of any US city but ranks 27th in population. Throughout the Seventies, Eighties and Nineties, the downtown and older neighbourhoods declined as people fled for the suburbs. By the 2000s city officials, notably former mayor Kirk Humphreys and current mayor Mick Cornett, began to raise funds to invest in downtown public realm and civic improvements. Still young people were moving to busier, booming cities like Austin, Texas.

Over the past several years, as the energy sector has rebounded, the quality of the city centre improvements and the affordability and attractiveness of Oklahoma City's older, close-in neighbourhoods have begun to attract young people priced out of Austin or Los Angeles back to the city. And reinvestment in high streets, in business start-ups and in small-scale residential development has followed.

This kind of grass-roots, small developer revival is happening in a number of smaller US cities, including Asheville in North Carolina, Nashville, Pittsburgh, Providence, Rhode Island, and Kansas City and Lawrence in Kansas State. Quality of life and quality of place, affordability and the ability for work to be more portable seem to be drivers of this trend, which results in both reuse of older buildings and in funky and authentic new buildings fitting into the urban grain.

My visit to the annual Congress for the New Urbanism meeting confirmed this trend. The new urbanists earnt their stripes rehabbing failed urban public housing estates as mid-rise mixed neighbourhoods and building new towns or big urban extensions. But the current work seems to be more about reviving urban neighbourhoods with streetcars, better street design and place making, as well as repairing failed suburban shopping centres, strip malls and business parks.

It's still hard to see the parallel to this trend here in Britain. Scrutiny of local plans reveals a preference for large-scale urban extensions proposed by volume builders, and all the political parties express some allegiance to new towns. Urban revivals of the organic nature of those in the US are rare, and regeneration seems to be struggling for a model after the collapse of the New Labour subsidies in the recession.

Yet the popularity of cities like Brighton and Bristol may presage a similar trend for younger people to choose locations outside but near London. And a review of neighbourhood plans—as compared to local plans—shows a clear preference for small sites for housebuilding and the kind of targeted improvement to villages and neighbourhoods that I saw in Oklahoma City and heard about from urbanists from other second- and third-tier cities.

The United States planning system, while sharing the same legal antecedents, has always been federalised and hence less top down than here in Britain. This has promoted mayoral entrepreneurship of the kind we are just now seeing from George Ferguson in Bristol, with devolution perhaps promoting similar entrepreneurial leadership. High-speed rail in the southeast is already having a ripple effect on coastal towns and creatives are leading the way there. As rail lines north and west improve and land values continue to explode in London, will we see a market-led revival outside of London in the near future?

Urban Recycling and Doubling-Up: How Cities Really Respond to Growth

Building Design

June 9, 2016

Almost everybody agrees that London has both a housing supply problem and an affordability crisis. The supply problem is demonstrated by comparing house building at its peak with the numbers generated today. And most seem to agree that supply shortages drive prices up, causing the affordability crisis.

But what if London had only an affordability crisis, and the supply numbers were an artefact of lobbying by house builders to ease planning restrictions on new housing projects and for government to stimulate demand through various incentive programmes? After eight years of demand stimulation and planning reform, the number of permitted developments is up, but the number of housing starts is much lower. By and large, in London the new starts are being sold into the investment market.

So supply increases but slowly as London's population continues to grow. Where are all the people going? We hear stories of garages and sheds crammed full of Eastern Europeans, of millennials sharing flats and of young people remaining at home with their parents longer and often returning. All this is used to demonstrate the need for more homes, but there is little correlation between the needs of this population and the units being produced by the house builders. Part of the answer must be to get local authorities building housing again, but another part of the story has to do with what I would call urban recycling.

The housing stock we will have in 20 years is primarily the housing stock we have today, and that stock is surprisingly adaptable. A look back at periods of rapid urban growth reveals that much population growth has been accommodated in existing housing stock. With Scott Bernstein of Chicago's Centre for Neighbourhood Technology, I have been looking at how various cities responded to periods of intense growth pressure or affordability problems, and a look at one of these cities is instructive for thinking about London today.

Washington DC during the Second World War grew from a population of 663,000 in 1940 to 881,000 in 1945, with a net migration of 49,000. The larger Washington region grew as well and for the metro region this was a doubling of population. At the same time, in order to dedicate resources to the war effort, the government had imposed restrictions on new housing production.

So the growing number of people coming to DC to help with the war effort were largely accommodated within the existing housing stock, by repurposing public housing as wartime housing and by "doubling up," with existing households being converted to flats and families taking in lodgers. DC authorities acted quickly to remove restrictions on rooming houses and on conversion of larger detached single family dwellings to multiple occupancy.

In many ways, it was a good thing that the Washington DC region met its wartime requirements through recycling and repurposing its existing stock, for the population quickly declined after the war ended and DC's population dropped by almost 200,000.

There is some evidence that housing demand is being met in London through the same means of "doubling up". According to Matt Hutchison at spareroom.co.uk, there are 19 million empty bedrooms in owner-occupied property in the UK, and last year saw a quarter of a million people advertising rooms for rent. London has the highest proportion of homes with six or more occupants and saw the largest proportional increase between 2001 and 2011 at almost 50%, according to the Office of National Statistics.

Allowing conversions of owner-occupied homes to accommodate lodgers or create an additional flat as permitted development would be a further incentive to put these empty bedrooms to use, generating needed income for many people with substantial equity in their homes but limited income.

At the same time, it is well documented that more and more families are living as intergenerational households, with adult children remaining in the family home for much longer. Again, the notion of allowing conversion of owner-occupied homes to accommodate a parent or a child as permitted development is a way to encourage urban recycling without allowing slumlords to develop substandard accommodation.

I have been as guilty of focusing on building new homes as a response to our affordability crisis as most experts, but I am increasingly coming to believe that cities are more resilient than we give them credit for, and that encouraging adaptation is as important as master planning urban infill and urban extensions. For architects, there will be plenty to do. Unlike volume house building where the engineer dominates, adapting individual homes is clearly the province of the architect and the small builder.

How to Diversify Housing Delivery With Some Help from Architects

Building Design

April 4, 2017

It is widely agreed that the dominance of the house building market by the volume house builders has distorted the market. It seems clear that a more diverse sector can only be of benefit to consumers, the economy and the architecture profession

Giving a larger share of the market to custom and self-builders is one of a number of ways to diversify housebuilding, along with building by councils and build to rent. Both the absolute number of small and medium-sized builders, and the number of homes they build, has declined since the recession. The number of self-build homes, where the home owner does much of the construction work and the custom-build sector, where an individual home is contracted with a builder/architect, also declined after the 2007 recession, from 14,000 in 2007 to 10,600 in 2013, according to a House of Commons briefing paper.

The recent Housing White Paper argues that a million people could be in the market for a self- or custom-built home. The proportion of self-built homes in England lags far behind Europe, with only 7–10 percent of completions as compared to 60 percent in France. In Berlin alone 190,000 homes have been constructed by self-build groups.

The government has attempted to stimulate self- and custom-building by making funding available through a Custom Build Investment Fund for schemes of five or more homes, and more recently through the recently inaugurated Home Building Fund. Obtaining mortgages has been a challenge, with a number of lenders dropping out, but at least 26 lenders now offer a product for custom or self-builders. The government has also acted to ensure that a proportion of government land released for homes goes to self-builders.

These actions appear to have had a limited impact, as availability of land and the complexity of the planning and regulatory process appear to be the two biggest barriers. The Self and Custom Build Act, given Royal Assent in 2013, addressed part of the land issue by requiring councils to maintain a register of interested self-builders. This has now been accompanied by 2016 requirements for "sufficient suitable development permission of serviced plots of land to meet the demand for self/custom build housing." This action promises to address the land availability question, which has in the past been exacerbated by the tendency of local plans to only allocate larger sites, for ease of administration and oversight.

The complexity of planning process is also a powerful disincentive to self-building, especially as planning departments have declined in size in recent years. Neighbourhood planning, which tends to allocate smaller sites, may be of some help. Of greater potential is the move in the Housing White Paper to create pink zones, "where local development orders or Development Corporations could give broad approval in advance for particular types of development."

But perhaps the biggest potential in encouraging self-build and custom-build is the architecture profession. Roger Zogolovitch and Martyn Evans have both called for hybrid architect/developers to meet the gap in the market. Architects are ideally placed to help clients with planning and building regulations on small sites. It is but a small step to identifying and assembling small sites for community groups, as is common practice in Germany and the Netherlands. Partnering with brokers to assist with mortgages is also manageable.

A group of U.S. architects and planners committed to development in the U.S. have formed the Incremental Development Alliance with a goal of cultivating 1000 small developers, and are holding "boot camps" to help people make the leap from designer to designer/builder. A September 2016 Small Development Summit attracted UK participants from both Massive Small and the Project for Lean Urbanism.

There has been debate in these pages about Ben Derbyshire's proposal for a London Housing Expo, aimed at demonstrating excellence in housing design across different London contexts. Such an expo could focus on self- and custom-building, helping to de-risk site allocation by London boroughs, introducing architects to potential self-builders, and demonstrating the variety of self-build options from the sale of serviced plots to self-builders, to the sale of shells for fit out, to community builds. The architecture profession can be at the heart of this movement as community architects were with the DIY housing effort in the Seventies and as Adolph Loos was with the wild settlers movement in Red Vienna.

Seeing Empty Homes as an Asset, Not a Liability

Building Design

June 23, 2014

Detroit has received worldwide attention as a horror story of a city in decline: blocks and blocks of abandoned homes, white flight to the suburban areas, the seeming collapse of an economy of skilled work, and the invention of something called "ruin porn."

Recently, the bankruptcy of the City of Detroit has warred for headlines with ambitious efforts to get the city back on its feet, spurred by the Kresge Foundation and other philanthropies and one entrepreneur who is helping bring back the downtown. From being an unalloyed tragedy, Detroit is becoming a crucible for testing new ideas about revitalisation.

When I visited there last October for a meeting on streamlining the process of urban development, there was ample evidence of both grassroots regeneration—a market economy springing up, and small businesses taking root—and efforts to combat decline by tearing down what was left of burnt-out neighbourhoods. I was pleased to meet architects who had become developers and entrepreneurs.

Just as in England, in many cases the cost of repairing abandoned properties was greater than their market value, and so the City of Detroit proposed massive contracts to raze areas of the city and return them to farmland.

Now comes encouraging news of a Detroit programme to take abandoned homes which can be saved into a land bank and then auction them off. The programme is coupled with forgivable loans for repairs. Auctions have already begun, with notable success, even as the city begins taking abandoned properties into the land bank for evaluation and possible auction. Many people are moving to Detroit as they see it as a place where it is financially possible to make a start with a home and a business.

The idea of auctioning off abandoned properties or selling them for a pound to people who commit to fix them up and live in them is not new. Baltimore had a programme in urban neighbourhoods that brought back the Fells Point area, and the Empty Homes Agency has successfully introduced such an effort in Stoke on Trent.

Nationally the number of empty homes has declined, according to the Empty Homes Agency, but many local authorities in the north and the Midlands are still experiencing increases in the number of long-term empty homes. Nationally, there were 635,127 in England in 2013. This does not include a large number of flats above shops in town and neighbourhood centres which are kept empty.

The government has dedicated attention to this problem, thanks to campaigning by the Empty Homes Agency and architect and presenter George Clarke, primarily through a £100 million grants programme for housing associations and community organisations. Most existing policy and guidance is focused on asking councils to work with property owners, or providing capital to allow agencies to purchase homes, but local authorities have extensive powers up to and including compulsory purchase and enforced sale.

The progress made in reducing the number of empty homes is encouraging but stops short of the kind of combined top down-bottom up effort that is beginning to have such an impact in Detroit. Rather than simply seeing empty homes as a tool for delivering some housing numbers, local authorities might see it as an opportunity to attract young people to come and start businesses. A regeneration strategy might combine an active programme to build a bank of empty properties, with efforts to simplify the regulations governing bringing them back into use as homes and live-work units, and access to capital, design expertise and training for repairs. Flexibility to allow people to live in one property and rent one or run another as a work space, would make it possible for many to afford to get on the housing ladder. Architects could become leaders of this effort.

The problem of housing in this country is not simply a problem of high prices in the South East, it is also about economic imbalance.

In an era of austerity, programmes which seek to encourage sweat equity, self-rebuilding and regeneration through business start-up should be preferred to top-down schemes. The national government could help by encouraging some local pilot projects and by studying programmes that have worked elsewhere.

Part 9.
About London

I have lived in London since Christmas 2004. My wife and I have raised our children in London, and we have all become British citizens.

I love London for its history, for the fact that the whole world is here, and for its parks, monuments and great buildings.

More and more, I fear that this is being swallowed up by a deluge of speculative building, and these pieces written over this period of change reflect that worry, and attempt to address it.

London's Tall Buildings Bloopers

Building Design

April 12, 2016

For a couple of decades at least, London architecture has been dominated by a generation of architects now in their 60s and 70s. Embracing the building as object, they earned their fame with buildings like Richard Rogers' Lloyd's Building, Norman Foster's Gherkin and City Hall and Renzo Piano's Shard.

Their hegemony has continued into this decade, even as the focus has shifted from earning a reputation for themselves to satisfying corporate clients. Along the way, these generations have earned Britain a reputation by creating iconic buildings around the world.

At home, though, the demand is for towers for investors, with over 400 in various stages of construction, approval or planning. By and large, these buildings are being built for a luxury market, and to a blueprint favoured by investors the world over. The towers emerging from design now are characterised by lots of glass, a sort of high-tech look and often a lack of integration with the street. They are of a sameness (despite their many odd shapes), driven by their need to fit the demands of a floorplate filled with luxury flats and a lift core and of commodification as global investment product.

The sheer number of towers, the lack of clear policy to create or shape a coherent skyline, and the poor design of many of them has generated much public and professional concern. The Skyline Campaign, as well as the London Mayor's Design Advisory Group recent report *Growing London*, has decried the poor quality of design in the avalanche of towers engulfing London. For me, the jury is out as to whether it is the product that is to blame or the design.

It is a curious thing, this design problem. For London is seeing a new spate of good architecture, with designers delivering buildings that are striking as well as contextual, contemporary as well as respectful of heritage, and imbued with inventive programmes and a plural use of materials and approaches. Walking down Piccadilly, one can see new buildings by Eric Parry and Robert Adam, both responding to a street of great modern and traditional buildings while staking their own territory with decoration and proportion. At King's Cross, new buildings by Demitri Porphyrios and David Chipperfield frame traditional streets and squares.

Over at 50 Bond Street, Eric Parry's new facade combines regular fenestration with metal panels, succeeding completely in the Louis Sullivan trick of making a glazed facade look solid and full of mass. Meanwhile, down New Bond Street a bit, George Saumarez Smith's Richard Green Gallery succeeds so well at the great game that it appears to have always been there, showing that the next generation of classicists not only know how to deploy the rules, but when to break them. In this group can also be found Ben Pentreath, Craig Hamilton, Hugh Petter and Liam O'Connor.

Much of this new architecture can be found in cultural buildings and in infill settings like Mayfair and Holborn. O'Donnell and Toumey's new LSE building creates a vital new public space for the campus and fit a difficult plot, uses brick and glass in a striking way.

Caruso St John's Newport Street gallery for Damien Hirst, reuses existing buildings while deploying startling massing in the new-build portion in a way that still embraces the pedestrian. Haworth Tompkins have contributed both sensitive new mid-rise housing for the Peabody Trust and cultural buildings including the temporary Shed at the National Theatre. Patrick Lynch is another talent, whose Zig Zag and Kings Gate buildings in Victoria begin to show what drama his firm might bring to a taller building.

This is a highly diverse set of practitioners but what they have in common is the ability to really look at the city around their site, to respond to the urban condition, and to use massing, materials and even decoration to complete a street or a square. This contrasts mightily with the prior generation, who began with the building and the plan, and so often saw the urban condition as something to be overcome with private streets, gates and pilotis, however much they opined about cities.

Sadly, one wouldn't know that the architects named above were busy adding to the quality of London's streets and squares from looking at the emergent skyline, for by and large they don't seem to be employed building towers for the investment market. One exception is Eric Parry who has been commissioned for a 73-storey building that looks like it will fulfil the requirements of having floor-to-ceiling glass, albeit with COR-TEN steel cross braces and a white glaze.

It would be nice to see more of these British architects get the chance to tackle some tall buildings, and perhaps then we would find out whether it is poor design or a poor brief and a poor product that is the problem with tall buildings in London.

A Towering Mess that the Government has the Power— But not the Will—to Address

Building Design

March 5, 2016

A report from New London Architecture reveals that 436 buildings over 20 storeys were approved or are being planned for London, provoking more than the usual consternation, coming alongside reports that the market for luxury towers was softening dramatically. This is one of the conundrums of property development: that investors and developers must embark on projects with long lead times with imperfect knowledge about the actions of their brethren.

The report found that 80 towers were under construction, that 223 had been granted planning permission, and that a further 114 were in the planning process. Of this number, 73% were residential, and most were in central boroughs including Tower Hamlets, Greenwich, Southwark and Wandsworth.

Only 19 towers were completed in London last year, suggesting that developers are accumulating planning approvals while the tower-friendly mayor and deputy mayor Eddie Lister are in charge. During their time, few proposals have been rejected, and every project called in has been given the green light. Forty-three tower applications were submitted and approved within a year, suggesting that the planning system is not to blame for the undersupply of new housing. A banked planning approval has the effect of raising land values significantly, making it difficult for mid-rise or family housing to emerge later.

This tower frenzy comes as the market for luxury housing in towers is softening. Up until now, developers have been predicting and investors getting double-digit returns for buying and flipping these properties, making them attractive investments, particularly for foreign investors.

New research by LCP reveals that land sales for premium central London property fell by 8% and sales were down as well this past year after some years of dramatic appreciation. Developers in Battersea, Nine Elms and Earl's Court are all reporting slowdowns in sales. LCP projects that the trend in this area will continue until the "new build" premium that attracts foreign buyers is eroded due to oversupply, with 22,000 units under construction or in the pipeline in this area.

The market for relatively more affordable properties, including houses, flats and terraces, remains robust. It is difficult to retrofit luxury towers built to attract the new-build investor to suit first-time buyers and families, as the underlying viability of these schemes is driven by appreciation in land values at the higher end of the market. As this premium disappears, we will most likely see both empty buildings and banked planning approvals waiting for a market upturn, effectively sterilising development in prime sites, as many of the planned towers are in larger masterplanned schemes like Nine Elms, Earl's Court and the Greenwich Peninsula.

This is a shame, for recent work by the mayor's design advisory group (MDAG), of which I am a member, found many unfilled market niches for housing. Our Ageing London report saw a potentially large market of older Londoners wishing to release equity from their homes and remain in London. They are not well served by either the luxury homes market or the first-time-buyer inventory. Not ready for sheltered housing, these economically and physically active older people want amenities, space for visiting family members and for their possessions, and accessible locations such as London town centres and high streets.

MDAG's Growing London report found that more than a quarter of new residential development was of greater density than permitted by the Greater London Density Matrix in the London Plan, and that greater housing diversity, including mid-rise and low-rise typologies, private rented stock, and specialist housing as well as a shift to smaller house builders and smaller development were needed to meet future demands. With 40% of new housing on public land, MDAG felt that government had substantial ability to make this happen, were a less laissez faire attitude taken.

Unless the GLA and a new mayor take affirmative action to shape the market, it is likely that we will experience a continued housing shortage and economic shocks as the tower boom becomes a tower glut, and construction slows down. It's time to use public land as well as public sector planning to shape the market to deliver the housing that London needs for the future, with housing seen as infrastructure supporting a robust economy rather than as an investment product. The MDAG reports go a long way toward defining this agenda for London's next mayor.

Just Because the Powell & Moya Site Is Available Doesn't Mean It's the Right Place for a Concert Hall

Building Design

February 17, 2016

The idea of a new concert hall for the London Symphony Orchestra and other classical music producers has gained currency in the last six months, after its new conductor Simon Rattle raised it as part of his discussions about moving back to London. The imperfections of Barbican Hall as an acoustic venue seem to be widely agreed and, after some time, Boris Johnson has become a supporter of the idea. The government has agreed to fund a business case for the new venue and there is to be a favourite site.

Official opinion has coalesced around placing the concert hall into the site vacated by the Museum of London's planned move to Smithfield's General Market. In an urban cavity hard by the Barbican, the site is both a traffic roundabout and something of a pedestrian island, accessed by the fragmentary high-level walkway that was to have replaced street pedestrian activity in the City in the Sixties. Location of the new hall would have to await the move of the Museum of London. With all this in mind, others have suggested an alternative venue on the north bank of the Thames at Blackfriars, opposite Tate Modern.

Now comes provocateur Leon Krier with his own proposal. Krier, a former associate of James Stirling, is perhaps best known as the designer of Poundbury for the Prince of Wales, along with a new town in Guatemala. What's perhaps less known is that his love for classical music may exceed his love for architecture and urbanism.

Krier proposes a site redolent with both meaning and urban importance along what Terry Farrell has called the Nash Ramblas. The proposed Nash Ramblas stretches from the London Zoo through

Regent's Park down Portland Place past All Souls Church and down Regent Street to Piccadilly and thence to Trafalgar Square and Buckingham Palace.

Krier proposes to site the new complex, which he calls the London Music Forum, on Park Crescent at the terminus of Portland Place and the entrance to Regent's Park. His elegant and typically lyrical site plan references both Nash and his own predilection for a playful classicism.

According to Krier, "a new concert hall, a chamber music hall, a state-of-the-art educational facility, practice rooms, restaurants and exhibition galleries can form a new urban ensemble that includes the complementary amenities required for successfully supporting the London Symphony Orchestra's mission." He also proposes a new Waterloo monument and a monumental portico to terminate the major vistas on the site.

With this proposal, Leon Krier reminds us that the siting of major cultural monuments is a decisive act in city making, and in the making of what Camillo Sitte called our collective memory. In linking the new music venue to Nash's master stroke to create urban coherence out of a succession of individual London estates, Krier joins contemporary London to its ongoing narrative.

This proposal stands in sharp contrast to the commercial opportunism that characterises most urban regeneration, which seems to deny London's essential character in favour of a kind of internationalism driven by the needs of investment portfolios. Cultural venues are seen merely as attractions or enhancements to commercial schemes and often seem dominated by retail and speciality food.

Whatever one thinks of the architecture, and I like the way it continues a conversation with Nash and neoclassicism, Leon Krier's urban proposal has challenged us to see the new home for the London Symphony Orchestra not just as a complex which can fill a conveniently vacant site, but as an opportunity to add a significant monument in a way that enhances London as a great city. This is what Nash did with Regent's Park, his grand boulevard and the planning of Trafalgar Square and is what post-war planners did with the Royal Festival Hall and the South Bank. Hopefully his counterproposal will be considered as the uplifting proposition that it surely is.

Old Street Will Need More Than Money

Building Design

January 10 2013

The government's announcement of a £50 million grant to regenerate London's Old Street roundabout and create spaces within it, including a "FabLab," to a concept by architect 00:/, was greeted with mixed feelings here in Shoreditch, where I have worked since 2005.

On the plus side, all agree that the roundabout and station are awful: one of the least pedestrian-friendly interchanges in London. If Jan Gehl, Ben Hamilton-Baillie or Andy Cameron had been announced to lead the design team I would have led the cheering. That said, what is "peninsularisation," and will it result in a lively, people-friendly place? Apparently the plan is to fund an "indoor civic space" on the island/peninsula. But will a big shed with advertising images extend the positive phenomenon of Shoreditch and Hoxton?

In my career, I have seen the birth of creative quarters in a number of cities and a few things seem to stand out: lots of young people; a vibrant nightlife; excellent accessibility; a location close to the city centre and public transport; old, undervalued buildings with smallish floor plates; an urbanism characterised by grit and a fine grain, as evidenced by masonry or warehouse construction; narrow streets and small blocks; and lots of cafés, bars and places to congregate, meet and work. Not much has been added to the list since the digital age: high-speed broadband, better coffee, perhaps… At the core is affordable, adaptable space in a place that attracts people with more ideas than capital. Shoreditch and Hoxton have remained creative despite rising rents because the small buildings are unsuitable for occupation by corporate offices or large-format retail.

The strategy of channelling startups into spaces managed by digital brands or by the government is something else. It is more paternalistic, akin to the way we have tried to respond to market collapse. In the heady days of regional development agencies, people hired signature architects to attract attention, pumped money in to lure investment, and created "enterprise centres." I am not sure that the "Silicon Roundabout" either needs or will respond favourably to this approach. Certainly Old Street roundabout could be transformed from traffic sewer into public space, as Tim Stonor has suggested, and pedestrian priority could be given to a network of adjacent streets. But the model ought perhaps to be to extend the Hoxton/Shoreditch urban conditions further east and to learn from the success of the Tea Building and Trinity Buoy Wharf, combining adaptive reuse and new spaces.

Co-working spaces are more like markets than serviced suites, and we should look at building types that prioritise small occupancies within buildings of high interaction—both with neighbouring streets and internally. The arcade springs to mind, or London's market buildings. A "peninsularised" Old Street station will have trouble meeting that test.

Rather than speculating about a jargonised digital future, perhaps those thinking about Silicon Roundabouts ought to look more closely at what has already worked and copy success.

We Need Real Homes, not Ivory Towers

Building Design

May 31, 2013

Many have observed that we are in the "urban century," and that over two billion more people will be living in cities by 2030. British architects and urbanists market themselves globally and, in the recession, many firms have survived by taking on overseas projects. Certainly, we have skills in design, urbanism and sustainability that can be of great benefit abroad.

Global urbanisation is viewed as a supply issue: can we build cities fast enough to store all of these people? The assumption is that we must do so through standardisation and mass production, pouring the new urban dwellers into a series of waiting vessels. Often this means reverting to the failed modernist planning idea of towers in the park, dressed up with landscape urbanism, but bearing an eerie resemblance to failed estates of the 1960s.

Another assumption is that global urbanisation is largely a developing world issue. But the globalisation of capital and investment and the emergence of a global cosmopolitan elite and middle class is reshaping developed cities all over the world, not just in India, Brazil and China. The desire for commodified investments is driving a standardisation of real estate models, and homogeneity is beginning to afflict cities worldwide.

Over the last year, I have seen the same concrete frame, steel and glass curtain-walled towers rising in Sydney, Melbourne, Auckland, Vancouver, Toronto and here. This boom is driven by investors seeking stable markets and low interest rates and, even in areas of high demand, many of the flats remain empty after sale.

Last week in Toronto, I heard of over 150 cranes working on sites, mainly for what are being called "faulty towers" of studio and one-bedroom glass-walled flats, sold off plan. The ubiquity of this building type seems to be driven by its familiarity to investors and agents.

Here in London, the top-end One Hyde Park is sold but largely empty. In the middle of the market, at both Battersea Power Station and the Heygate Estate, overseas investors have bought much of the stock off plan—and it seems unlikely that the homes being built in London will satisfy the demand for housing for Londoners. Since the time of the Urban Task Force, planners such as Richard Rogers and Ricky Burdett have called for cramming more people into London with these kinds of buildings, arguing that density is the key to sustainable living.

Putting aside the fact that sustainable density can be achieved just as easily through street-based buildings, one doubts whether tall buildings that are occupied only part-time are making London more sustainable.

A market driven by investors seeking studios, one- and two-bedroom flats may fail to produce the housing England needs, and we may have another generation of unadaptable buildings, coupled with a shortage of affordable homes.

Aldo Rossi famously said the city is the collective memory of its inhabitants. I fear we are eroding our heritage and identity as we reproduce the same buildings globally. Surely British architects and urbanists are up to the challenge of building densely, and well, reflecting local identity in non-trivial ways?

Bigging up Battersea: a Progress Report

Building Design

December 11, 2014

Battersea Power Station is one of the longest-running development stories in London. For years it seemed an inevitability that the site would be redeveloped and that the power station and its chimneys might be lost. I wrote in these pages in 2012 about the importance of keeping Battersea Power Station and the challenge of developing a viable scheme that satisfied all of the desired planning obligations for the area. I worried that no developer would be able to develop a scheme that both met planning obligations for the area and reused the power station itself.

Of course events proved me wrong. A Malaysian developer outbid other contenders for the site, accepted most of the planning conditions and took forward a scheme to develop the site, with more than 1,000 residences already sold and a total of 3,992 approved along with three hotels. The first phases of the development are being followed by a third phase with buildings by Foster & Partners and Frank Gehry. The buildings respond to a masterplan by Rafael Vinoly, which programmed a curving pattern of new buildings rising to the level of the power station roof, leaving only the chimneys soaring above the surrounding development, except along the Thames itself. Peter Rees, former chief planner for the City of London, and since retirement a critic of overdevelopment, has called the project a disaster.

Now comes Bjarke Ingels' design for the area linking the Foster/Gehry projects with the southern entrance to the power station, called Malaysia Square in honour of the developers' home country. Among other things, BIG's design has to resolve the grade difference between a podium-level pedestrian street in front of the new buildings and the entrance to the Power Station. In developer speak, the new square does this by creating an "urban canyon," not something I have ever thought to be a good thing. Ingels wraps his design with a lot of rhetoric about Malaysian landscape to justify a grade separation that celebrates concrete and granite, has some improbable arches and sheer drops, and will probably be health-and-safetied and value-engineered into another bi-level pedestrian interchange with railings and ramps like so many that failed in the heyday of the street in the sky in the Sixties and Seventies.

It is easy to fault the architects, whose metaphorical ambiguity and tall tales have clearly got the best of them, and who have produced a sculptural thing that accentuates the problem with the urbanism. But the issue is clearly one of masterplanning, of allowing the over-scaled Foster and Gehry blocks to use a podium level rather than a ground level, thereby putting the power station entrance into a hole. It is further a planning fail, as the combination of viability arguments after the Malaysians paid so much for the site with planning obligations has created a context that envelops Battersea Power Station in a sea of buildings that will obscure the power station behind a dense series of hedges of residences and hotels.

What price conservation is the next question, a question that is posed every time a landmark is sold for a price reflecting high underlying land values, and the new owner bets on maximising value by squeezing more buildings on the site than land owners unburdened by conservation issues. Architectural writing now has to be as much about planning and economics, because in late-stage corporatism buildings have become product types, and planning has become assessment of fees and gate keeping. We have kept Battersea Power Station, but at what cost?

Are We Serious About Estate Regeneration?

Building Design

January 20, 2016

Estate regeneration and replacement is hardly an obscure subject, but it was still a surprise to see David Cameron devote both a speech and a column to the subject this week. When he did so it catapulted what has been a fairly non-partisan ideal into the trench warfare of political conflict.

In fact, Tony Blair made his first significant speech on the Aylesbury estate, which is only now being redeveloped. During the Blair years estate renewal was called New Deal for Communities, incorporating both physical and social strategies. A financial model involving developer participation in market properties and cross subsidy emerged, albeit with significant public funding for public realm, infrastructure and housing.

Over the past few years estate renewal has seen renewed attention in the press and among the profession, with debates over demolition, projects like Park Hill in Sheffield to improve rather than demolish, and high-profile London schemes at the Packington Estate and Heygate Estate. At the Heygate Estate, while there will be more than 2,500 units built, the number of social housing units was reduced from 1,194 to 632 and many of these will be shared-equity rather than social-rented units. Many residents were "decanted" (removed) and have not yet been able to resettle in the area. This has generated protest, especially as developers have attempted to reduce the proportion of affordable housing on viability grounds.

The group Create Streets has brought the issue of estate renewal to the attention of the government and the government has responded, beginning with a London commitment of £150 million. Cameron's intervention heralded a nationwide programme, with a commitment to tackle 100 estates across the country and commit £140 million to the effort. Calling for demolition, Cameron focused not only on improving the physical environment but also on improving "life chances" for residents.

The same questions are being asked of this scheme as have been asked of the Heygate estate. Jeremy Corbyn has called it social cleansing and challenged Cameron to demonstrate that the programme will result in a one-for-one replacement. On the other side of the ledger, Savills has estimated the potential for an additional 54,000 to 360,000 homes, depending on density, from comprehensive redevelopment in London alone. It argues that the value uplift from a Complete Streets approach is greater than other contemporary regeneration models, improving viability and hence potentially allowing the delivery of more affordable units.

Both the promise and the threat may be overblown, however, as the entire programme is allocated only £140 million, which won't go very far across 100 estates. By way of comparison, the US Hope VI effort, begun during the Clinton administration to replace failed social housing estates with walkable, mid-rise and mixed-use schemes, has expended more than $6 billion in the years that it has existed, tackling just over 200 projects. Current funding for what is now called Choice Neighbourhoods is reduced due to budget constraints, but ranges between $90 million and £120 million, devoted to planning grants and two to three projects per year. Clearly the £140 million should be an annual amount rather than a total.

Proponents argue that the funding shortfall can be made up from the value uplift and residual from building at higher density and building homes for sale on the private market. While this may be attractive on paper, one can already imagine the viability consultants sharpening their pencils to demonstrate that one-for-one replacement is not financially viable. Indeed local authorities have been ill-prepared to respond to viability analyses or even to release them for public scrutiny.

If the government seriously wants to tackle the issue of estate renewal, it needs to dedicate substantial multi-year public funding to ensure the replacement of existing social units, to enact a replacement guarantee, and to require a community-led process to ensure that what emerges reflects the community consensus rather than a developer-driven approach of higher density without a walkable street pattern. Doing this might result in a realistic programme with a chance of success.

London's Housing Problems are Beyond the Power of Market Forces to Solve

Building Design

August 25, 2015

Understanding what is happening in housing in London means understanding that London is a world city, subject to market pressures well beyond the boundaries of the Greater London Assembly. Increasingly, this means that Londoners looking for a home to rent or buy are at the mercy of forces well beyond the simple ones of supply and demand of housing for other Londoners.

At the top end, developing new London housing has become an increasingly attractive investment proposition for foreign investor/developers, from Malaysia and China to Qatar. By and large, these investors are interested in the high end of the market, and this drives the supply of new housing toward the top end. Often these properties are themselves marketed as investments to be bought off plan and flipped on completion for a tidy profit. At the same time, the luxury end of the market is increasingly dominated by foreign buyers.

All of this drives prices up, as does the continuing attractiveness of London as a dynamic, stable and safe world capital. The supply imbalance towards the top end of the residential market further stresses the middle.

Both the pressure from the upper end of the market and the lack of substantial growth in the affordable sector have meant that more and more Londoners are renting privately. The proportion of Londoners in the private rented sector has grown from 26% in 1993 to 40% in 2012. All indications are that private renting will continue to be in demand, as young people are increasingly unable to afford homes and as London remains a magnet for people from Europe to come and work.

But London is affected globally in another way as well, as an attractive city for tourism, and this has begun to affect the property market as well. The advent of Airbnb has given property owners another way to capitalise on the value of their property and has likewise been a boon to travellers seeking a more economical, personal way to experience another city. Interestingly, Europe is Airbnb's largest market, with 58% of its listings.

The growth in short-term rentals through Airbnb has generated controversy, with Barcelona's mayor attempting to manage the impact of short-term visitors on people in the city's residential blocks. In San Francisco, a city dramatically changed by Silicon Valley and gentrification, evidence that some property owners have evicted tenants to put their property on Airbnb has generated outrage. The Anti Eviction Mapping project has mapped the proliferation of short-term rentals in the city.

The excellent open data site Inside Airbnb has recently done the same thing, along with some useful analytics for a number of cities, including London. Using Airbnb's own listings, they have discovered that there are 18,436 listings in London, and that over half of them are entire homes or flats. 86% are available more than 90 days per year, and over half of Airbnb listers have multiple listings. The data confirms what any Airbnb user has long known: that most units are being maintained as short-term rentals, and that increasingly this is a profitable business for many property owners,

As Airbnb's popularity begins to grow, more people will buy flats for the purpose of short-term letting, and there will be a tendency for landlords to consider shifting to short-term tenancy when tenants move out. This year the government has made it easier for property owners to do this legally, and I for one wouldn't necessarily want to constrain what someone does with a flat they purchase.

The pressure on housing stock is undeniable, and when combined with the other factors affecting London supply it leads to the conclusion that it is highly unlikely that market forces and subsidies to stimulate buyers will solve London's housing shortage. Developers will continue to supply what they wish, the private rented sector will continue to be stressed and without a grant programme or enforceable affordable housing planning conditions, "affordable" housing will not be produced in large numbers. Without subsidy sufficient to allow local authority or housing association investment in housing, it seems to me London's affordability crisis will continue to worsen as the city draws in foreign capital, buyers and visitors in growing numbers. And I fear that this building programme needs to embrace not only homes for the poor, but working Londoners as well.

Part 10.
From Place to Place

I spent many years in transportation planning and development, as a public-transport planner, an airport director, and as an advocate for greener modes of travel. Looking back on these articles, I see a consistent effort to reframe transportation not as an end in itself but as a means to an end: access to jobs, homes and society, greener and more sustainable cities and towns, a cleaner environment.

A Greener, More Pleasant Vision for Travel and Transport

The Ecologist, 2009

People have always moved to cities for opportunities, and cities have always been places where jobs and services are concentrated. The inherent advantage of cities is accessibility to other people, to goods and to services—what might be called location efficiency. People travel fewer miles by car in cities, consume less energy per capita in cities, and providing them energy, water, transport and food if more efficient than in suburban or rural settings.

Particularly in the United Kingdom, our ambivalence about cities has led to a tradition in planning and development which sought to marry the advantages of urban life—convenient transport, good jobs, reliable power, water and services—to the ideal of life on the manor or in the village, with trees, capacious gardens and housing standing together in a manner isolated from work, shops and schools. The Town and Country Planning Act promoted the separation of uses into distinct districts connected by roads optimized for speedy travel by car. This was called zoning, and in pursuit of quality of life, it has tended to destroy the inherent environmental advantage of urban living, as it has forced travel by car to accomplish the daily activities of our lives. And so the suburbs, which sought to merge the best of urban living with the best of country life, have resulted in cancelling out both.

As a result, transport is a growing part of the climate change problem. As emissions from other sectors of the economy have declined in recent years, transport's carbon emissions have continued to grow from 14 percent of Great Britain's CO_2 emissions in 1980 to 23 percent by 1997. According to the UK's Environmental Accounts, "household use of private vehicles" accounted for 40 percent of greenhouse gas emissions in the transport sector in 2005.

Automobile by-products including brake and tire particulates, air toxins and pollutants and road chemicals, run off into groundwater and are increasingly acknowledged as a major source of both ground and surface water pollution. And impervious surfaces like roads and pavements prevent rainwater from percolating into groundwater, leading to increased levels of runoff into canalised river systems, and increasing flooding risk.

The recent *Foresight Tackling Obesities: Future Choices* report by the Government Office for Science looked at the alarming rise in the incidence of obesities in Great Britain, concluding that by 2050 60 percent of adult men, 50 percent of adult women and about 25 percent of all children under 16 could be obese, leading to increased chronic disease risk from diabetes, stroke and coronary disease and economic costs to society and business of over £49 billion in today's dollars. The report concluded: "human biology is being overwhelmed by the effects of today's obeseogenic environment, with its abundance of energy dense food, motorised transport and sedentary lifestyles. Indeed, although doctors recommend 30 minutes of moderate physical activity per day, the actual amount of time Britons spend walking and cycling has declined from 12.9 minutes in 1995–6 to 11.8 minutes in 2005–6, a decrease of 8 percent in just a decade. The Foresight report concluded that there might be a win-win solution: "Many climate change goals would also help prevent obesity, such as measures to reduce traffic congestion, increase cycling or design sustainable communities."

Signs of Change
All is not gloom and doom, however. In the past decade it is possible to see that progress has been made in providing greener travel options and getting people to use them. While London has led the way in shifting consumers toward public transport, walking and cycling, there are is a Europe-wide trend toward increased intercity passenger rail travel, and there is some evidence of a decoupling of economic growth from its long relationship with growth in travel by car.

Pioneering projects such as Poundbury, the Prince of Wales's own development with the Duchy of Cornwall in Dorset, have shown that mixed use, mixed income development centred on walkable neighbourhoods can succeed in the marketplace.

Poundbury challenged conventional paradigms for street design, reducing widths and sight distance, eliminating road signs and forcing drivers to respond to the urban environment rather than tailoring the urban environment solely for the car. Its innovations and similar efforts by English Partnerships with The Prince's Foundation at Upton and elsewhere, have informed the Department for Transport's new "Manual for Streets," which incorporates many of these ideas.

A step beyond the notion of once again making walkable streets and neighbourhoods is the idea of developing communities at public transport hubs, to improve access and reduce the need to drive for work or shopping. The Northstowe "ecotown" outside Cambridge, promoted by English Partnerships and designed by Arup, is aligned around a rapid bus system, as is the Sherford New Community, designed by The Prince's Foundation and Paul Murrain.

A Look at London
London has been in the forefront of cities dealing with sustainable transportation globally, due to both its leadership in proposing congestion pricing, and improvements in London's bus services. At the same time, London has England's most widespread and accessible public transport, its areas of greatest density and a street network that precedes the development of the suburban cul de sac system.

One only needs to compare the share of total trips by public transport between London and other British cities to learn that greater London is starting from a much higher base. In Great Britain as a whole, two-thirds (64 percent) of all trips are taken by car, as compared to London, where less than half of all trips (43 percent) are made by car.

Trans-European Networks: A Revival of Rail Travel
The long-awaited arrival of the first Paris train into St. Pancras station in London awakened many to the renaissance in high-speed high-quality passenger rail service on the European continent. This growing network is reducing journey times and improving connections all

over Europe, and it is coming about as a result of European policy. The shift has been promoted in order to provide a realistic alternative to short-distance air travel, as air trips under five hundred kilometres are far more damaging than longer trips, due to the greater emissions from the take off and landing cycles. Over shorter distances high-speed rail competes well in terms of both time and convenience with air travel, and may be superior in terms of the quality of the journey.

As a result passenger rail use has been growing across the European Union, but the United Kingdom rail patronage per inhabitant lags behind that of other leading European nations. Germans travel 865 rail passenger-kilometres per inhabitant each year, the French travel 1,231-rail passenger-kilometres per person annually, while the average UK resident travels only 674 rail passenger-kilometres per annum.

Rather than extending the European high-speed rail network beyond St. Pancras station to the north and to the west, government policy has tended to focus on dealing with commute overcrowding and extending station platforms. While it is clear that improving the performance and capacity of existing services is critical—achieving a step change in rail use and a shift from short distance air travel and car use to rail travel will necessitate integrated thinking and planning.

Demand for rail travel is projected to grow by an additional thirty percent over the next ten years. In fact, in the last decade the rail system has regained all of the passengers it lost in the forty years since Beeching's cuts.

Looking Ahead
What's needed are a linked set of policies and investments to promote not only greener travel modes such as public transport and cycling, but also the reduction of the need to travel through location of many of one's daily needs within walking distance and trip substitution through telecommuting. Such policies would include:

- Linking transport and growth, so that new housing should be well served by public transport, and within walking distance of shops. New communities or eco-towns must be located at major

public transport hubs, and built around the concept of walkable neighbourhoods.
- Congestion and road pricing should continue to be a key tool, not just for the purpose of lessening congestion but for the purpose of supporting the shift to greener travel modes and the reduction of the need to travel through land use strategies and travel behaviour change programmes.
- Programmes to reduce the energy consumption of rail, bus and tram should be undertaken along with programmes to regulate fuel economy, both through vehicle technology fixes and changes in driving behaviour.
- The growth in rail travel should be continued, with expansion of high-speed rail systems from Europe into the UK, including both a north-south high-speed link from St. Pancras and service from London to the West. Public transport links to outer London stations should be considered to relieve bottlenecks coming into central London, and incremental improvements in speed and capacity should be continued, along with major investments in stations.
- Strategies to improve the walkability of existing neighbourhoods and introduce mixed use should be implemented alongside programmes to retrofit existing buildings for energy efficiency. It is essential to reduce carbon emissions from both buildings and transport.
- Travel behaviour change programmes, already being piloted by government, should accompany all new commercial and residential development, with introductory information and public transport discount packages provided to new employees and incoming residents alike. Studies have shown that the most effective interventions in travel behaviour occur immediately after relocation.
- The greenest travel modes are walking, cycling and avoiding travel altogether, and programmes need to be in place for these modes too. The creation of continuous cycle networks, interconnected walkable streets, and the encouragement of flexible

working, job sharing, and satellite and home-working all will play a major part in this change toward a networked, sustainable city.

There are a series of stark choices ahead of us. As the evidence about climate change has mounted, it has become ever clearer that the time for action is now. Common sense would dictate dramatic improvements to the overtaxed networks for rail, public transport and cycling funded from road pricing or carbon taxes.

What's needed is courage and leadership. As we have seen, the vision for the urban environment is one in which quality of life is improved rather than degraded, and the changes are ones which can improve one's interactions with family, with colleagues and with community. The alternative can also be clearly seen: crowded roads and trains, longer commutes, and higher costs to fix the problem if we fail to act.

Why We Can't Afford to Miss the Train

Building Design
November 22, 2013

I have often argued for fewer grand projects and a more fine-grained architecture and urbanism. But one place where big projects and systems thinking are needed is infrastructure, for it sets the framework for investments in place. So I am inclined to believe in investment in high-speed rail and airports, and argued for an extensive UK network in *Transport and Neighbourhoods*, my 2008 book with Edge Futures.

High-speed rail, as a part of an overall transport system, can enhance the transport experience, stimulate regional economies and divert traffic from car and air travel.

But the more I look into HS2, the more I worry that it is being driven by engineering and cost-benefit analysis—leaving the core social and economic reasons for the investment out of the design equation. Not only does this undermine the case for HS2, it means that the project may fail to achieve the potential benefits.

Transport investments can help unlock access to land, permit more intense development and enable households to make different housing choices. This can transform regional economies, if it is part of broader land-use transportation strategies. Making cost-benefit decisions primarily in terms of the effect of reduced travel times is too narrow, and allows the debate to be reframed negatively as a choice between noise and environmental impacts on neighbourhoods and the countryside and travel time savings for commuters with laptops.

A few people have recently offered perspectives that see transport investment as a tool to address housing affordability and regional competitiveness. If the debate can be reframed in this way, the question is no longer should we build HS2, but what HS2 should we build?

Peter Cuming's proposal for Euston station shows that design matters, by putting connectivity and related development over first cost. Michael Heseltine's idea to create urban development corporations around stations would capture the value created by improved access, creating a vehicle for providing needed housing and allowing the regions to create development strategies that will make them more successful. And many have called for better connections to airports and HS1, and to what is amusingly called the "classic" rail network.

Many rail advocates have looked at HS2, seen its flaws and concluded it should be dropped. I fear if we don't move forward now, nothing will happen for a generation, and we can't afford to slip further behind. We must find the will to advance high-speed rail and airport investment in London. But both need to unlock and capture the value of the shaping power of transport.

Alongside a more broadly framed transport investment, government must use its powers to assemble land, create a friendly yet directive framework for private investment and thus enable the transformation. Architecture and urban design are critical here, for the project-driven approach will seek to save costs by cutting connections, simplify delivery by ignoring synergies, and reduce complexity by partitioning "outside" issues like value capture, user experience or placemaking into another project. What's needed is not more analysis of the benefits but an HS2 that recognises the centrality of these issues to project delivery and success.

Beauty Isn't a Dirty Word

Building Design
November 9, 2016

John Hayes has long been a minster with interests beyond the normal range for politicians. When he served as the skills minister he took an interest in craft by sponsoring a craft prize with the Crafts Council and dropped by the Prince's Foundation's summer school to take part in a life drawing class. In his earlier term in transport, he expressed an interest in improving the quality of design and introducing local food at motorway service stations.

Now he has got attention and received a fair amount of kick-back by arguing that transport design should embrace beauty as one of the goals. His speech was followed by a similar appeal by Oliver Letwin on flood defences this week.

Hayes has riled architects by committing at least three cardinal sins: citing the Prince of Wales, quoting philosopher Roger Scruton and decrying brutalism. This last point flies in the face of the current campaign to reconsider brutalism and overturn the popular feeling that these buildings have not performed well over the years. Articles such as Felix Salmon's Why Brutalism is Back in Style posit that these buildings, far from being ugly as most have said, are actually beautiful if one appreciates their starkness and texture, particularly in photographs on Instagram.

This argument takes one back to one of the old debates about architecture. On the one hand, architects and culture writers argue that judging the aesthetic fitness of a building requires an education, and an understanding beyond that of the ordinary person. Indeed, the popularity of the Barbican as a middle class and professional residence supports the notion that one can be educated to appreciate these well-made buildings, however gross their intrusion on the urban landscape.

Beauty is believed by many to be entirely subjective and—worse—old fashioned. And the argument for brutalism turns on the idea that starkness, massiveness and the use of raw materials can transform ugliness into a kind of beauty, when viewed from the right angle.

John Hayes argues that people know beauty and ugliness when they see it, and that the clear popular consensus in support of traditional and vernacular buildings represents an understanding about beauty that is rooted in natural forms and rich in detail. He argues that beauty is a thing of universal human value, citing Plato, Hegel and Burke. And this leads in turn to the idea that, as the most public of the arts, everyone, regardless of their level of education, has a stake in architecture and the city.

The campaign for brutalism has emerged in part because many of these buildings were threatened, and I have to support the idea that the best of them need to be saved, particularly if they have not failed as useful buildings. But John Hayes' speech comes at a time when proportion, sensitive use of materials, detail and even ornament are being accepted back into British architecture, as this year's Stirling Prize award demonstrates.

Hayes argues that this trend should extend to transport architecture, for it will dominate public spending on infrastructure in coming years. Projects such as Blackfriars Station, cited approvingly by Minister Hayes, and John McAslan's King's Cross departure concourse, have demonstrated that the marriage of engineering and architecture can be inspiring and beautiful, as the Victorians demonstrated at Paddington, Liverpool Street and St Pancras.

All too often what one sees in motorway and rail architecture is functionalism that doesn't soar and the use of concrete and steel without an eye to transcending the limits of the materials in the ways that the best bridges, terminals and embankments can do. HS1 from St Pancras to the Chunnel is a case in point, as the concrete structures seem like nothing so much as a scar on the landscape.

John Hayes' call for beauty in transport design should be welcomed by architects, as there is huge room for improvement (and lots of work in it for the profession). HS2 cuts through beautiful countryside and urban areas on its way north. Surely we can envision designs which enhance the urban and rural landscapes in the way that Brunel's Great Western Railway or Foster's Millau Viaduct have done so well?

Highway Capital and Economic Productivity

Originally published in *Progress* (Washington, DC: Surface Transportation Policy Project), Spring 1999. Revised in 2003 for Reconnecting America

At the national level, two basic arguments have been made to advance the thesis that highway investment is good for the economy. First, the addition of highway capital stock is said to make it easier for goods to be delivered quickly and efficiently, thus reducing transportation costs for private companies and enhancing their productivity and presumably that of the nation. The second argument is that highway investment leads to good jobs in the highway construction and supply industries, as well as has a ripple effect through those workers participating in the goods and service economies of the nation.

Each of these arguments is used to advance the thesis that increased highway capital investment and a bigger highway network are good for the economy, an argument that is flawed on its face. After all, the fact that eating one dinner is good for you doesn't lead everyone to the conclusion that eating two dinners would be better, does it? Beyond this obvious flaw, the arguments for greater highway investment to stimulate the economy do not hold up under scrutiny. We'll look at each argument in turn.

Highways and Productivity
First, an efficient highway network is said to reduce transportation costs for private firms, enabling them to compete better, enhancing their profits and productivity, and thus, presumably, the nation's productivity. This was one of the key original arguments for the construction of the Interstate system, which indeed did connect the nation and enable cheap transportation by truck virtually everywhere in the

country. The Federal Highway Administration commissioned a major study of this question in the early Nineties, looking at data from 1950 to 1989 to ascertain the savings provided by the highway system to the private economy. The study was updated recently to include data from 1990 and 1991. It should be noted that the rates of return estimated in the FHWA study ignore the costs of externalities such as air and water pollution, costly sprawl development which follows new highways and costs to the economy associated with death and injury on the highway. At the same time, however, they ignore the consumer benefits of highway expansion.

The study found a positive annual average rate of return for highway investment, with much greater rates of return in the early years of Interstate system construction. However, according to a review of the original study by the Congressional Budget Office, "benefits diminished over time as the highway network expanded. By the 1980s the overall stock of non-local highway capital was only four percent below the size beyond which further increases would cost more than they would return in benefits to business."

In fact, the study update completed last year found that the rate of return has continued its precipitate decline, from .54 in the 1960–69 period of rapid Interstate development to just .09 in 1991. According to the Congressional Budget Office this is below the 11 percent return to private capital, making additional highway capital not an attractive investment.

This declining rate of return would tend to suggest that this country has enough highway capital stock, and that additional highway capacity is unlikely to yield substantial economic benefits. This makes sense. The high rates of return in the sixties and seventies came from the construction of our network, and represent the benefits of network access to firms throughout the economy. These type of network impacts are unlikely to occur again, although benefits might be obtained from investments to network our highway, rail and aviation systems together.

A corollary finding would be that reinvestment of the 52 percent of capital outlay dollars now invested in new capacity to maintenance and rehabilitation of existing highway capital stock might yield significant economic benefits. FHWA's own benefit cost analyses support this argument, showing much higher benefit cost ratios for reconstruction projects than for new capacity. The Congressional Budget Office concluded that, "beyond a certain point, maintenance and management of existing infrastructure become(s) more attractive than investment in additional capacity, which becomes more costly." From a national perspective, then, we ought perhaps to be directing federal resources to rehabilitation and management of our highways, not to new capacity, which appears to have a lower rate of return than not collecting the taxes. And even within reconstruction, highways may not be the best investment. Clark Wieman, Research Director of Cooper Union's Infrastructure Institute, estimates the per passenger capital costs of reconstructing transit to be one-tenth those for highways.

Jobs, Jobs, Jobs
The second major argument for increased investment in highways is that they are a good source of jobs. In a recent article in *TR News*, Madeline Bloom and Nancy Bennett of the Federal Highway Administration estimate that every billion dollars invested in highways supports approximately 42,000 jobs, and they cite a ripple effect as highway workers spend their wages in the economy. While highway construction clearly requires labor, how many jobs and at what cost has been the subject of some lively debate. For example, a recent University of Illinois study of the economic impacts of the controversial I-69 highway proposed in Indiana found that each job generated would cost $1.5 million, compared to $5,000 to $30,000 per job in rural economic development programs.

The argument that highway construction generates employment and that such employment generates economic activity is only meaningful if road building generates more employment and economic activity than other types of public expenditure. In fact, Wieman estimated in *Technology Review* that new building projects or major construction generate 40 percent fewer workers than do road maintenance projects.

Investment in transit can also be expected to generate a higher level of employment due to the continuing need to operate public transportation systems. Transit is simply more labor intensive than highways. In fact, studies for the Economic Policy Institute found that benefit-cost ratios for transit exceed those for highway spending. If the reason for public investment in highways were simply to generate employment, then other more labor-intensive public sector areas such as education or public safety would clearly outperform highway investment.

Getting Past the Hyperbole
Clearly continued federal investment in the highway system is necessary from an economic perspective, if only to protect our enormous sunk investment in highway capital. A careful review of the research reveals, however, that investment in new capacity does not appear to generate a positive return, and that federal investment ought to focus on maintenance, rehabilitation and management of our highway system. A significant return on investment might be generated from networking our transportation networks together through targeted investment on intermodal connections.

Yet we continue to invest heavily in new capacity and major new highways are proposed around the country, with wild claims for job creation and economic impact. As *Fortune* reported in 1996. "Are the new highways really necessary? David Forkenbrock, director of the public policy center at the University of Iowa, says the US highway system is adequate, and suggests that economic gains will flow more from what type of goods are made than how those goods are transported.

Says Forkenbrock: 'To say you need a better or more capacious highway is silly rhetoric.'"

Testimony before US Senate Commerce Committee in Air and Rail, 2003

US Senate Committee on Commerce, Science, & Transportation

AMTRAK

April 29, 2003

Chairman McCain and members of the Committee, thank you for the opportunity to appear today to discuss Amtrak, and the future of passenger rail in this country. I am Hank Dittmar, Co-Director of Reconnecting America, an independent initiative to define a new national approach to inter-city travel for this new century. We believe that passenger rail can play a significant part in our nation's transportation system, if we redefine the role that intercity rail plays in that network, and if we provide stable levels of capital funding, create incentives for connecting our separate air, rail and bus networks together, and remove regulatory barriers that prohibit coordinated planning and integrated approaches to delivering intercity transportation services— both passenger and freight.

Intercity passenger rail can play several important roles in an integrated long distance travel network: it can relieve airport and highway capacity in congested corridors, it can provide an important alternative in case of system disruption, and passenger rail is more energy efficient and climate friendly than either short haul air transportation or travel by automobile. The public supports an expanded intercity rail program. A 2001 national survey by the United States Conference of Mayors found that 69 percent of those polled supported an expanded higher-speed rail program in the nation. It is ironic, though, that even as support for intercity rail grows, and its importance to the nation is increasingly recognized, Amtrak's future seems less secure than ever. The reason goes back to Amtrak's creation.

Amtrak was never meant to succeed, and it has fulfilled that expectation. When Amtrak was created as a publicly owned private corporation in 1971, it was saddled with an impossible set of conditions.

These conditions included:

- An expectation that it could operate without public subsidy, something the private railroads had failed to do with passenger service, and something at which no passenger railroad in the world has succeeded;
- An inherited set of routes that served the major population centers of the 1880s, and that the private railroads had failed to succeed with, once lucrative mail contracts were transferred to the airlines;
- A political expectation that all of the cities on the network would continue to receive service, regardless of population density;
- A franchise allowing Amtrak to operate on freight railroad rights of way at incremental cost, something the private railroads believe causes them to lose money on each Amtrak train;
- A board that often lacked the necessary expertise to support the Corporation's challenging mission;
- Annual appropriations battles for general fund revenues for both capital and operating uses, placing them at a severe disadvantage when compared with aviation, highways and transit, all of which enjoy the protection of a trust fund and multi-year funding.

On top of these familiar problems is a problem not unique to Amtrak: the failure of United States transportation policy and practice to approach transportation service delivery in a networked manner. Each mode—air, rail, bus, automobile—is presumed to operate independently, and to compete with one another for customers and scarce resources. The failure to network the transportation system, with both public and private components, is increasingly leading to system and market failures within each industry, and these failures are increasingly threatening continued improvements in our Nation's economic productivity.

Finding a solution to Amtrak's dilemmas involves tackling this problem head on. All other solutions are suboptimal at best, involving only damage control. Whether private entities or quasi-public entities operate Amtrak, or whether infrastructure and operations are separated is likely to matter little, unless a fundamental shift in the role of passenger rail is also accomplished in the context of the ongoing rationalization of the airline industry and of freight transportation.

That we are experiencing a crisis in intercity transportation at this time can be demonstrated by citing a few examples:

- The continuing problem of metropolitan congestion, resulting from the concentration of commute travel on the Interstate network, threatening its viability for the intercity transportation of passengers and freight;
- The ongoing decline in the number of airline passengers and the related series of airline bankruptcies, resulting in a restructuring of the hub and spoke system in a way that leaves many small and medium-sized cities with little or no air service. According to the Air Transport Association, air travel under 250 miles is down over 25 percent, trips between 250–500 miles are off 15 percent through the second quarter of FY 2002, while longer trips are off less than 5 percent.
- The continuing high levels of subsidy for Amtrak's long distance trains, along with a crisis of unfunded infrastructure on the Northeast corridor.
- The shrinking of the railroad network, and the finding by the Surface Transportation Board since its founding in 1996 that the private railroad industry has failed to make back the cost of capital in a highly capital-intensive industry.

These are not new problems, but they are reaching a tipping point where government action is needed to ensure stable and reliable interstate commerce. I do not believe that the proper response is a series of continued episodic bailouts of Amtrak, the airlines, and the road industry, however. Rather, the country needs to integrate our systems and rationalize the market through a combination of: continued deregulation, removal of barriers to intermodal investment, dedication of capital resources, and a new vision for intercity travel the scale and scope of President Eisenhower's Interstate system. This time, instead of routes within a system, it should be connections between the systems.

Unless this happens, many cities will be cut off from the long-distance travel network, forcing more long-distance trips onto highways and further degrading the performance and reliability of that over-stressed system. Reliable freight transportation enabled improvements in logistics and the creation of the just-in-time manufacturing system. These developments have been key to the large gains in productivity that have enabled economic growth over the past two decades.

These gains in productivity are being eroded as highways become more congested, especially in corridors where highway capacity cannot be added, as airport congestion and airline restructuring erode both the performance and the accessibility of the aviation system, and as a lack of reliable connections between ports, airports, highways and rail networks in metropolitan areas diverts freight onto highways, rendering its on-time arrival less and less predictable.

The elements of a solution are beginning to emerge across the country as states are beginning to take on partnership roles in intercity passenger rail, cities and airport authorities are creating "travelports," linking air, rail and intercity bus into one convenient facility, and private operators are experimenting with intermodal code sharing, airport express bus operations, and integrated rail-bus scheduling. The next step is to take the promising examples that are emerging, and build a coherent federal policy framework that allows their replication at a national scale.

Some of the promising developments that are emerging around the country include:

Innovations in Surface Transportation Modes: The distance from 100–400 miles is the most effective market for intercity bus, commuter rail and intercity rail. When airport access, waiting, security and transfer times are taken into account, bus and rail become cost- and time-competitive within this range.

Three kinds of markets exist for rail and bus in these distances: for airport access in lieu of an auto trip, from city center to city center in substitution for an air journey, or to substitute for the spoke portion of a hub-and-spoke journey or for an auto trip.

Across the country we have seen several success stories for intercity rail in these kinds of markets. They stand in marked contrast to the overall performance of intercity rail, and typically they involve partnerships between Amtrak and the state, wherein the state invests in equipment, track and station improvements and provides service subsidies. For example, the recently inaugurated service between Boston and Portland, Maine created a new rail market compensating for a loss of airline seat capacity from Portland of 26 percent from 2000–2001.

Other partnerships are occurring on the West Coast. In California, increasing rail service on the Capitol Corridor rail line—to nine trips each way daily between Sacramento and Oakland, California—increased ridership by 40 percent between 2000 and 2001 and freed up both air and highway capacity. Capital Corridor ridership exceeds a million riders a year now. More Amtrak service improvements supported by the state of California resulted in record ridership levels on other California rail corridors. The California experience also points up the value of intercity bus links with rail, where buses are scheduled to meet trains to transport passengers to communities not reached by the rail network.

Another important step is improved equipment and service quality. Introduction of the sleek Talgo trains in the Pacific Northwest in 1999 boosted ridership between Seattle and Portland and reduced travel time by more than a half-hour. The state–railroad partnership (the states of Oregon and Washington and Amtrak and BNSF Railway) is planning steady improvements to track and terminals to increase speed and frequency with the goal of carrying quadrupling ridership from the 2001 level of 565,000 annually by 2016.

Turning Airports into "Travelports:" The idea is to turn airport terminals into travelports where rail, bus, and urban transit would be added to the traditional mix of aviation, parking and rental cars. By making selected improvements to provide more reliable service options via other modes of travel for short and medium-distance passengers, airport capacity will be freed for the higher-value, longer air trips. This kind of system is also more redundant, in the positive sense that travelers are presented with more options when regular service in a single mode is interrupted. A more redundant system is also an investment in economic security to ensure continued movement in the face of natural or man-made disasters. The value of this was clearly shown in the Northeast Corridor in the hours and days following the September 11 disaster; many studies also documented the ability of rail transit to provide continued service in the wake of the California Loma Prieta and Northridge earthquakes.

This solution also provides a way to address the revenue problem airlines confront as business travelers respond to declines in service by seeking low-fare, no-frills carriers by providing an increase in value.

There is still a place for carriers that provide services that people value at a higher price. The only question is how much these services can take advantage of intermodal integration. Linking European planes with trains has been focused on business travel markets, like Frankfurt–Stuttgart or Paris–Brussels. By offering downtown access on fast train connections, airlines can charge high-yield fares for high-quality service, about the only alternative to today's focus on low-fare, low-yield strategies.

Conventional wisdom says the European experience cannot be replicated here, because distance between cities is greater, and because it is too difficult to make the air rail connection happen. We looked at intercity travel in the United States and found the distance between most metropolitan travel markets is within that range. For instance, the distance from Chicago to Detroit is 284 miles, from Los Angeles to San Francisco is 400 miles, Portland to Seattle is 187 miles, from Dallas to Houston is 250 miles, and from Miami to Orlando is 234 miles. The fact is that half of scheduled commercial air trips are less than 500 miles and almost that many are less than 400 miles in length.

In fact, innovative airport rail and bus connections are being made, and we have begun at Reconnecting America to assess the potential at key airports around the country. Our analysis reveals that it is feasible to connect the surface rail and bus networks with the aviation network at 54 key airports around the country, and that many cities are in fact trying to make the connection, despite numerous institutional, financial and legal barriers. A few examples serve to illustrate the very real potential.

- Newark International Airport: the Newark Airtrain connects the airport with NJ Transit and Amtrak's Northeast Corridor at a new Newark Airport station, where ticketing and check-in facilities are available. Continental and Amtrak are now code-sharing.
- Ted Stevens International Airport, Anchorage: a new station and covered pedestrian connection has opened recently between the airport and the Alaska Railroad.
- Burbank Municipal Airport: the Burbank Airport is directly served by the Metrolink Commuter Rail, with ten daily trips and the Amtrak's Pacific Surfliner with four daily trips. Amtrak's Coast Starlight passes through the station but does not stop.
- San Francisco International Airport, where a fourth station of the BART regional rail system to the airport will terminate in a joint BART and Caltrain commuter rail station at the airport. The station, which will open in late June 2003, will also accommodate a future high-speed rail line which is on the statewide ballot for approval this November.
- Baltimore Washington International Airport: a light rail line from Baltimore directly serves the terminal, and a bus shuttle connects with the BWI rail station, which is served by Amtrak and the MARC commuter service. This is one of the fastest-growing stations in the Amtrak system.
- Key West International Airport, Florida where an intermodal terminal connects air service with Greyhound bus service and with an Amtrak thruway bus.

There are some 21 air-bus connections in the country, but many airports actively discourage bus terminal facilities.

In addition to these examples, airport intermodal projects are in the planning and development stages at Chicago's O'Hare International Airport, with a commuter rail and possible Amtrak connection and a direct high-quality transit express connection in the works; at Providence's T.F. Green airport, with a combined rail station and rental car facility; and at Miami International Airport, where an intermodal station is planned. Notably, Dallas–Fort Worth International Airport, following the success of the Metroplex's light rail and commuter rail investments, is planning to connect both systems directly into the airport. And our discussions reveal that there is some active planning around this concept at most if not all major hubs.

The key actions needed are the following:

- Focus Intercity Rail Primarily on Short and Medium Distance Markets: Recognition that the restructuring of the airline hub and spoke system away from shorter-distance spokes creates an opportunity for intercity and commuter rail and intercity bus to serve markets between 100–400 miles. Amtrak should cease to be primarily an operator of long-distance train routes, and should instead focus on the short- and medium-haul markets where it can be competitive with both highway and air travel.

Two interesting examples of underserved markets for passenger rail are in the Southwestern United States, where the Los Angeles to Las Vegas corridor and the Phoenix to Los Angeles market are prime candidates for rail service... Congress should create a dedicated capital program for service improvements in intercity corridors linking city pairs under 400 miles that serve markets in excess of a minimum threshold of total one-way trips per year by all modes. Funding could be provided to states on a matching basis to encourage the creation of partnerships between Amtrak and state governments.

- Provide for An Essential Transportation Service Program: In order to create a truly national Interstate Highway Program, as well as a National Plan of Integrated Airport Systems, Congress has always subsidized transportation facilities and service in less dense corridors with funds derived from more densely populated areas. Such subsidies have been justified in terms of equity, in terms of the economic benefit to smaller communities, and in terms of national connectivity. They have also been widely criticized for economic inefficiencies, overly high per-passenger subsidies, and diversion of funds from higher priorities. It is likely that as long as there is a federal system and a United States Senate, these arguments will continue. At the same time, though, it should be possible to reduce costs, increase accountability and provide improved service to the rural areas of the West and the Great Plains by pursuing an intermodal approach.

Instead of individual programs, Congress should create an Essential Transportation Service program, distributed to the states, which would allow the subsidization of rail service, intercity bus service, or air service based upon a finding of cost-effectiveness as measured by population provided accessibility, frequency and convenience. The program would need to recognize that air service is point-to-point service, while rail and bus can serve entire corridors, often on a multistate basis. The aviation reauthorization legislation recently sent to Congress by the Bush Administration takes a good first step in this direction, by reforming the Essential Air Service program to provide for ground transportation services at short and medium distances.

- Create a "Last-Mile" Intermodal Connections Program: This would be a new intermodal funding category, funded by a series of modal funding sources with authorizations of $1.5 to $2 billion per year to fund projects to eliminate bottlenecks and make intermodal connections. Direct grants, loans and credit enhancement would all be funded. Eligible projects would include: intermodal terminals at airports and downtown hubs incorporating intercity rail and bus and local transit, and connections to the system; similar terminals and connections at ports, intermodal freight bottleneck relief in congested metropolitan areas and key corridors, and incentive grants for merged information, baggage handling and ticketing.

Freight bottleneck relief projects should demonstrate an enhanced rate of return for the freight railroads.

- Eliminate Legal Barriers To Intermodal Passenger Transportation Services: Current airport, highway and transit statutes all act to inhibit creative action by states and metropolitan regions seeking to make airport intermodal connections. The barriers are fiscal, institutional, and regulatory. The first action is thus to untie the hands of airport proprietors, metropolitan planning agencies, state departments of transportation and transit agencies seeking to connect their airports to the surface transportation network.

If necessary, federal laws should be modified to allow alliances and mergers between intercity carriers in different modes, to encourage air-rail or air-bus and bus-rail networks to merge.

- Intermodal Policy and Planning: Build on the metropolitan planning capacity being funded for highways and transit by requiring rail and aviation plans to be coordinated with the metropolitan plan and the state plan, as appropriate. We applaud the Administration's recommendation in their Aviation reauthorization proposal to link proposed aviation investments with the metropolitan surface plans. Their proposal also includes a provision to create an intermodal information demonstration, which is an important and essential part of an integrated, networked approach to intercity travel.

Intercity passenger rail is an essential part of a forward-looking national transportation policy. At the same time, we need to reform the way we approach passenger rail, just as we need to rethink our approaches to other transportation modes.

An authorization which provides stable multiyear capital funding, promotes partnerships with states and private entities, creates incentives for intermodal integration with intercity bus and aviation, and refocuses Amtrak on primarily serving short and medium distance travel would be a big step in the right direction.

Sprawl, The Automobile and Affording the American Dream

From *Sustainable Planet* by Betsy Taylor,
Juliet Schor, Karl Steyaert

Copyright © 2002 by The Center for a New American Dream
Reprinted by permission of Beacon Press, Boston

In 1998, there were 184,980,187 licensed drivers in the United States, and 207,048,193 licensed motor vehicles. For many decades, transportation analysts warned of the economic impact of the saturation of the domestic auto market as the ratio of drivers to cars neared one to one.

But the nation reached the supposed saturation point, and kept going. Now we view cars as lifestyle objects, and need multiple vehicles for our many faceted lives—or our many faceted fantasy lives. In 1995, 91 percent of all US households owned at least one car, and 59 percent of all households owned at least two cars. The wealthier a household is the more vehicles it owns. In 1995, households with incomes under $20,000 owned an average of 1.3 vehicles, while households with incomes over $80,000 owned 2.4 autos. Rising motor vehicle ownership is also encouraged by government policies. The federal government has subsidized the construction of roads and highways, kept gas prices low, and, with pressure from special interest lobbies, greatly limited the availability of alternative modes of transportation.

In 2000, Ad Age magazine estimates that the seven largest automobile manufacturers spent over $11.9 billion on advertising for new cars, while the United States government invested only $7 billion on mass transit systems. As a result of relentless automobile advertising and equally persistent assaults on public transit by rightwing groups opposed to all things remotely public, auto ownership is associated with wealth, style, physical prowess, daring and sexual conquest, while transit use, rail, biking, and walking are seen as either public bail-out systems or dangerous and degrading activities. I find it curious that we subsidize the auto industry to the tune of billions of dollars while public investment in high speed rail, metropolitan subway or bus systems are decried as failing programs that should survive on no public funds.

During the last forty years, the country has experienced an explosion in auto use, especially during the years from 1960-1980; when the United States embarked on the program of highway construction called the Interstate system. The federal government offered states 90 cents for each 10 cents they contributed toward the construction of a national highway network, and the result was an increase in paved road mileage from 1.2 million to 2.4 million miles from 1960-1998. Total lane miles grew even more dramatically, especially on urban freeways. During the same period, driving grew by over 300 percent, or an average of 9.6% per year.

These highway systems, coupled with a change in zoning codes and street design fostered by federal agencies dramatically reconfigured the nation's urban landscape, making it harder to get around by train, bus or foot. The new highways penetrated the cities, destroying homes and disconnecting neighborhoods from one another. The early increase in vehicle use was seen as a function of the growth in auto ownership, driver licensing, and population; but it is clear that the increase and improvement of highways played a large part as well.

In recent years it has become clear that suburbanization has contributed to the growth of driving. As people spread out into far flung suburbs, two things happen: commuters must travel longer distances to work, school and shopping, and each of those activities becomes more spread out. Thus, the average household stayed roughly the same size from 1983 to 1990, as measured by the Nationwide Personal Transportation Survey, but its auto travel grew by about 12,000 miles per year. Over the same period, the length of the average work trip grew from 8.5 miles to 11.6 miles, as sprawl has moved home and work farther apart. Catherine Ross and Anne Dunning examined land use factors in the National Personal Transportation Study and found that both auto ownership and miles driven per adult increases significantly as population density declines. So we have a classic case of a system out of control, where the provision of physical infrastructure to accommodate travel has stimulated consumption of both vehicles and travel, which has in turn stimulated sprawl, which then causes a demand for more highway infrastructure.

In recent years the growth in travel has been accompanied by a decrease in vehicle efficiency and an increase in harmful emissions. A two-decade trend toward better fuel economy has been reversed, and average miles per gallon of the US auto fleet has declined in the past five years as consumers responded to heavy advertising and began to purchase light trucks and sport utilities, with their higher profit margins for manufacturers. These vehicles now comprise more than half of new sales each year. Dramatic improvements in tailpipe emissions of ground-level pollutants brought on by clean air regulations are being offset by increases in driving. As to gasoline consumption and carbon emissions (which are the main problem for global climate change), we are seeing dramatic declines in efficiency. But the Corporate Average Fuel Economy (CAFÉ) standards haven't been changed since the Carter Administration, and indeed Congress and more recently the Bush Administration have blocked any improvement of these standards, continuing to exempt light trucks and sport utility vehicles from efficiency requirements. The car companies have exploited this loophole.

The impacts of so many Americans driving more and bigger vehicles are profound.

More than one-third of US carbon dioxide emissions and 40% of Nitrous Oxide emissions come from the transportation sector. These emissions have contributed to a host of health problems. Recent reports by scientists from the Centers for Disease Control link sprawl and driving to increases in asthma mortality and to a precipitate decline in physical activity, which is in turn a factor in growing rates of heart disease and childhood obesity.

Automobile byproducts including brake and tire particulates, air toxins and pollutants and road chemicals, run off into groundwater and are increasingly acknowledged as a major source of both ground and surface water pollution. At the global level, Americans consume more than one-third of the world's gasoline. For every gallon burned, approximately 19 pounds of carbon dioxide are emitted to the atmosphere, contributing unintentionally but dramatically to melting ice caps and a host of threatening problems tied to global warming.

By some estimates, one-third of our cities are devoted to the automobile in the form of streets and parking lots. Over 41,000 Americans die each year on highways, and Americans are more likely to be killed as pedestrians than they are to be killed by a stranger with a handgun.

In fact, autos are the leading killer of the nation's teens. A recent National Research Council report estimates the annual costs of death and injury from automobiles and highways at $182 billion, an annual amount equal to the total cost of building the Interstate system.

Our Appetite for Consuming Land – A By-product of Auto-Dependency?

A recent survey of planning experts and historians found that the most significant planning action of the past century was the construction of the Interstate Highway System, for it made possible the suburbanization of America. In many ways suburbanization has had a positive influence on American life. Prior to World War II, many urban dwellers lived in overcrowded conditions, with inadequate ventilation, poor emergency access, little heating and substandard plumbing. The post-war housing boom largely solved those problems.

But suburbanization also unintentionally caused the rapid loss of farmland and open space, destruction of vital habitat for hundreds of plant and animal species, increased air pollution and climate change, and weakened the fabric of our communities and neighborhoods. In part, this is because the availability of the automobile and the creation of metropolitan highway networks has made it possible for people to live farther and farther away from work, school and shopping. In part, suburbanization is due to the exploitation of cheaper land on the urban fringe made accessible by the highway network, and so families choose cheaper housing farther out. Zoning and traffic codes from the 1920s and 1950s, which legislate against mixed land uses and force rigid separation between housing, work and shopping activities, have made the problem worse.

The Impact on Household Budgets
The consumption of transportation has a major impact on household budgets for all Americans. The American Automobile Association estimates the annual cost of owning and operating an automobile at $7,363 in 1999. About 75% of that cost is fixed costs such as car payments and insurance, and this means that there is little financial incentive for drivers to drive less once they made the investment in a car. Nationally, transportation expenditures account for 17.5% of the average household's budget, according to an analysis of Bureau of Labor Statistics data by the Surface Transportation Policy Project and the Center for Neighborhood Technology. The proportion of household expenditures that is devoted to transportation has grown as our use of the automobile has grown, from under 1 dollar out of 10 in 1935 to 1 dollar out of seven in 1960, to almost 1 dollar out of five from 1972 through today.

The transportation burden borne by American households falls most heavily upon the poor and lower middle class, as the less a family makes, the more of its budget goes to transportation. The poorest quintile of American households spend 36 percent of their budgets on transportation, while the richest fifth spend only 14 percent.

This means that the poorer a family is, the less money it has available for other expenses such as housing, medical care or savings. In fact, transportation takes up the second largest percentage of the household budget, ahead of food, education, medical care and clothing, only behind expenses for housing.

The cost of transportation varies widely from region to region, and within metropolitan areas. Scott Bernstein and Ryan Mooney of the Center for Neighborhood Technology recently analyzed data from the Consumer Expenditure Survey from 1998-9 and their work revealed that transportation costs can vary from 14 percent of a household's total expenditures in the New York Metropolitan area to as much as 22 percent in Houston.

These differences between regions are due to land use differences. (The difference between New York and Houston would have been greater had not the New York metropolitan area as defined by the Bureau of Labor Statistics included the suburbs of New Jersey.) Research at the metropolitan level done by John Holtzclaw and others shows that sprawl accounts for the difference in transportation costs by forcing an over-reliance on the automobile and by necessitating longer trips. This study which analyzed odometer readings collected as part of air quality inspection and maintenance programs, found that residents of denser, transit rich neighborhoods drove far less and spent far less on transportation than people who lived in more sprawling suburban locations characterized by single use zoning.

The Impact on Wealth Creation
The growing proportion of consumer expenditures that is devoted to transportation inhibits families from devoting their income to saving or investing, and indeed may be part of the reason why so many families have to send two people to work. For the fact is that spending on transportation by poor families, unlike spending on home ownership or investing in education, has a very poor return on investment because autos, unlike houses, are depreciating assets. Ten thousand dollars invested in a car declines to a value of about four thousand dollars in ten years' time, while investment in home ownership builds equity and often appreciates. Similarly, investment in college education for one's children increases their earning power over their lifetime. The fact that the poorest families must spend over a third of their income on transportation means that they are least able to invest in activities that offer them the opportunity to build wealth. It is indeed ironic that many progressive social scientists believe that the best way to help former welfare recipients secure jobs is to give them automobile purchase assistance, thereby trapping them into the poverty cycle even more profoundly, as the poor typically end up with less reliable cars which are more expensive to operate and maintain.

The Way Out—Encouraging Trends
That's the bad news. The good news is that Americans are increasingly fed up with the bad choices they have been offered, and growing segments of the population are demanding homes on smaller lots in neighborhoods, where walking is safe and pleasurable, and amenities are within walking distance. This shift in preference is being seen by

developers, builders and elected officials, and they are beginning to respond by building mixed-use neighborhoods, reviving urban neighborhoods and walkable suburbs, and building dozens of new transit systems.

Growth in Driving Flattens; Transit Use Is On the Rise
One of the most hopeful signs is that over the past two or three years, the upward slope of the driving trend has begun to flatten, even as population has continued to rise. The rate of growth in driving has dropped from 3% per year in 1998 to a slight decline in 2000.

At the same time, public transit ridership is increasing. Transit's heightened popularity comes against a much smaller base, partially due to the fact that public transportation is only available to about half the population, and available and convenient for a much smaller percentage. Transit use grew 11% from 1998 to 2000, according to ridership statistics collected by the American Public Transit Association. Much of this growth was concentrated in cities where lots of transit service was provided like New York City and Chicago, but 2000 saw significant ridership increases in cities in nontraditional places too. Bus ridership grew in Oklahoma City by almost 8 percent, in El Paso by over 13 percent, in Oklahoma City by almost seven percent and Spokane by seven percent from 1999 to 2000.

Some of this growth in transit use is due to the fact that transit agencies are learning to make riding more convenient for the passenger by offering multi-ride smart cards, but much of it is due to the fact that transit is becoming more available as the roads become more congested. New rail systems are proliferating all over the country, with new rail lines opening in the past decade in places far from the transit rich East Coast such as St. Louis, San Jose, Denver, Los Angeles, Dallas, Portland, Salt Lake City, Sacramento and San Diego. All of these cities have met or exceeded patronage forecasts, and all of them have plans underway to expand their systems.

New transit systems are in the planning or construction stages in a host of other metropolitan areas around the country including Houston, Seattle, Minneapolis-St. Paul, Phoenix, and Tampa. Most of these new systems are commuter rail or light rail systems, although a growing number are busways or rapid bus systems. Both types offer the rider the option of a vehicle that has time advantages over the private motor vehicle, either because they don't have to share the roadway with cars, or they are given preferential treatment at traffic signals.

Living Downtown – A Growing Trend
One of the other recent trends that may indicate a move away from the growth in consumption of land and auto use is the growing number of people who are choosing to live in downtown areas. A recent study by Rebecca Sohmer and Robert Lang for the Fannie Mae Foundation and the Brookings Institution found that 16 out of 24 downtowns surveyed had grown in population from 1990 to 2000. While this trend is still small in comparison to the number of households choosing to locate on the periphery of metropolitan regions, it may be an indicator of people's willingness to live in denser areas. Indeed, downtown areas are increasingly seen as places to live, not just as places to work and shop. Sohmer and Lang argued that the desirability of downtowns is due to their proximity to work, mass transit and amenities and that this proximity augured well for a continued growth in downtown populations, and for perhaps a spillover into adjacent urban neighborhoods.

One of the downtowns to have experienced the most growth in Sohmer and Lang's study was Chicago, which grew in both downtown population – by almost 50 percent in the decade from 1990 to 2000 – and in density.

Private Markets Are Responding
This growing trend back into more compact, walkable, mixed-use communities is being driven largely by consumer preferences in the marketplace, and not by government action. Increasingly real estate developers are seeing an untapped market in providing new housing types. Heralded as the "new urbanism," this visionary development has attracted architects and builders, because it is beginning to offer an attractive alternative to urban sprawl. The New Urbanism also provides a comprehensive template for development that appears to

attract a premium in the marketplace according to the Urban Land Institute. Hundreds of New Urbanist developments are open or underway across the country.

As a consequence, real estate forecasters and investment experts are advising their clients to invest in mixed-use communities, and companies are showing a preference for these kinds of developments. A recent study by Jones Lang LaSalle of so-called New Economy companies found that access to mass transit was a very important factor in location selection for 77% of companies surveyed.

The annual Emerging Trends in Real Estate report, which rates all types of real estate investment in differing metropolitan areas, advises investors to select locations characterized as "24 hour cities," with mixed-use development and access to transit. Investors are cautioned to avoid investing in projects in suburban locations without access to transit, as growing congestion makes these risky investments.

The private marketplace has also seen a growing trend toward transit-oriented development, which is located and designed to take advantage of proximity to mass transit. Transit-oriented developments are located within easy walking distance of a transit facility, contain a mix of uses including housing, services and retail, and are designed to make driving unnecessary for many trips. Often spurred by local government investment in transit, these kinds of developments are finding easy acceptance among consumers. One developer in the Portland, Oregon area put it this way: "We had 46 sales in the first four months, which is the highest absorption we've ever achieved for a new product in the Portland market."

Even those living in dense urban neighborhoods have an occasional need for an automobile. In response, a variety of schemes for car sharing have emerged in Europe and the United States. Typically a variety of cars are purchased and distributed throughout neighborhood locations, and car sharing customers or members are able to access them within an easy walk or bus ride of their home, in contrast to auto rentals, which are concentrated at airports and in downtown locations. Car sharing, which is being offered under a number of different business models, including hourly rental and member cooperatives, is moving rapidly into the American market. A recent survey found that car-sharing programs were being introduced in about a dozen American cities including Chicago, Seattle and San Francisco, and that car rentals were also considering adding the hourly rental feature to their product lines.

Some lending institutions are also changing loan criteria to reflect changing consumer preferences and needs. The Location Efficient Mortgage (SM) a product of Fannie Mae and a consortium of groups called the Institute of Location Efficiency, allows prospective homebuyers in denser transit-rich neighborhoods to use their transportation savings to help them afford a home in these neighborhoods. The program, which has been introduced in Chicago, Seattle and San Francisco, is expanding to Atlanta, Portland and Philadelphia, and Fannie Mae has announced plans to introduce a less comprehensive product with smaller savings in Minneapolis-St. Paul and Baltimore. In essence, financial institutions are now sending a message – if you save money by driving less, we'll take that into account and offer you more funds to purchase a home.

Changing Demographics Mean Changing Demand
These products are responding to changes in consumer preferences. Cities, once stigmatized as crime-ridden repositories of the poor, are now being seen as vital, resource-rich places, in part because increased density creates the opportunity for a more diverse mix of amenities than is available in one-dimensional suburban locations. A larger trend lies just underneath this change in attitude, though. The demographics of the country are gradually shifting, and these shifts portend a fundamental change in the demand for housing and community. There are four interrelated demographic trends underway, which have been dramatically illuminated in the 2000 Census results. Each of them holds the possibility of helping us move from suburban sprawl and traffic nightmares to reinvigorated urban centers with high quality of life.

IMMIGRATION
The most notable finding of the 2000 Census was the unequivocal diversity added to our nation as a result of immigration from other

countries, principally Hispanic and Asian households. Historically, most immigrants and most minorities live in cities, and while there is a significant trend toward minority migration to the suburb, demographer William Frey projects that most immigrants will continue to be concentrated in more dense urban locations. This urban concentration along with the lower income levels of most immigrant households has historically meant that these households own fewer automobiles and drive less. According to Catherine Ross and Anne Dunning's analysis of the 1995 National Personal Transportation Survey, African-Americans, Asians and Hispanics are all more likely to use public transit or walk than Whites. For immigrants, this may be due not only to income and poverty level, but also to cultural factors, including the fact that they have lived in places where transit use was the norm rather than the exception. As immigrants assimilate into the population, therefore, we can expect to see higher levels of driving as incomes rise, but also a continued willingness to use public transit, particularly if its availability, quality and convenience continue to increase.

"Empty Nesters" and "Echo Boomers"
The second demographic trend is the aging of the baby boom generation, and its passage from the child rearing stage of the life cycle to the "empty nest" phase. Families that once demanded the single-family home on a quarter acre parcel in a suburban location are now finding both the home and the location to be unsuited for a new stage of life.

Evidence suggests that baby-boomers have fueled much of the downtown population growth over the past decade, as they seek smaller homes in locations with a greater mix of amenities.

Marketing experts and demographers alike have trumpeted the Echo Boomers' (aged 24-34) preferences for exciting, dense, urban locations. Indeed, the much-publicized growth of new economy cities like San Francisco and Austin was ascribed to their attractiveness to highly skilled young workers. A recent study found that 57% of this generation preferred small lot housing and that 53% felt that an easy walk to stores was an extremely important determinant in housing and neighborhood choice.

Non-Family Households
The 2000 Census found that non-family households comprise 31.9% of all American households, more than married couples with children at home, a group, which now comprises only 29.5% of households. Ross and Dunning found that single adults with no children, and households of two or more adults with no children were most likely to live in urban locations. These less conventional households are another force for positive change.

The Shift in Housing and Neighborhood Preferences
These demographic trends add up to a growing market for smaller homes, town homes, and homes on smaller lots, and a desire for more lively walkable neighborhoods. In a recent study released by the Congress for the New Urbanism, Dowell Myers at the University of Southern California estimated that between 30-55% of the demand for new housing would be for residences in dense, walkable neighborhoods. He also found that almost 25% of the aging baby boomer demand was for attached housing (townhomes) in the city.

Meeting the Demand – The Role of Public Policy
If we hope to contain and even reduce the number of miles Americans drive alone each year, we must first acknowledge that the auto will remain the single dominant mode of travel for the foreseeable future. The automobile is convenient, reliable and cheap. At present, most Americans do not have a choice not to drive for most of their trips. Walking or bicycling is difficult if the streets lack sidewalks or if shopping, schools and libraries are inaccessible. Public transit is often not within reach, and when it is, it often is more expensive than driving and less frequent than is convenient. The cities and suburbs where most of us live are structured around the automobile—our zoning codes, financing systems and tax laws encourage developers to build single family homes on large lots which are physically separated

from daily activities. Originally these laws were meant to protect us from smelly factories, but now they separate us from a loaf of bread, from the hardware store, and the elementary school. A multifaceted approach to this problem is essential—an approach that gives Americans a choice not to drive rather than an approach which seeks to punish us for driving. At the same time we need to build consciousness about the need for improved efficiency and Detroit should be required to offer more fuel-efficient vehicles at all levels of the automotive fleet.

In large part, the effort to reduce driving is also an effort to restore communities to places we'd like to live and share in, rather than transient places to build equity. Creating livable and walkable communities where transit is an option can increase our access to opportunities and amenities, serving a variety of ends. A shift to these kinds of communities can help families build wealth, as less income is devoted to depreciating assets like cars, and more is available for home ownership or saving for education. At the same time, these diverse, mixed-use neighborhoods are more interesting, and families will find that the less time they spend commuting or carpooling children around the more time they have for their children.

Giving Americans the Choice Not to Drive

What will it take to make this vision a reality: to reduce driving and improve efficiency in a manner that increases opportunity and enhances quality of life? A truly sustainable system will require a variety of positive changes. There are a host of policy reforms that could move us in the right direction. These include home mortgages reflecting reduced expenses from living in a dense, transit rich neighborhood. Or tax policy that provides as favorable treatment for people who bike or take transit to work as it currently does for those who get free parking from their company. A collaborative national effort by the American Planning Association has just been completed to develop new zoning and planning standards, which favor mixed-use development that is less auto-dependent, to replace the old standards that have brought us the suburb. Government would do its part by locating government facilities and service in transit oriented communities, by linking affordable housing subsidies to such communities and by encouraging its workers to telecommute. Over time, these changes would result in the development of communities that are accessible by more than automobiles, where transit really works and where neighborhood businesses reduce the need for much travel.

At the same time we need to build the infrastructure that makes all this possible.

The 1991 Intermodal Surface Transportation Efficiency Act and its 1998 successor TEA-21 have already provided cities, suburbs and states with the opportunity to invest in travel options other than highway development. Under this federal law, local governments can opt to allocate federal transportation funds to any number of transportation options, from bike paths to hybrid electric buses. Increasingly they are doing so, as they realize that to cure congestion in the suburbs by widening roads is like trying to cure obesity by loosening one's belt. In the near future, affordable, frequent, reliable bus or rail transit will be a short walk away in the central parts of our major cities and "smart" shuttles and vans are a phone call and a short wait away in our suburbs and smaller cities and towns.

Walking should be an option, with pedestrian routes no longer being considered a hindrance to car travel. A network of bike trails, paths and lanes would be almost ubiquitous, using available rights of way in streets and abandoned rail corridors. The federal transportation law is up for renewal in 2003, and this presents an opportunity to do more to encourage states and localities to invest in transportation facilities that encourage community livability, make walking and biking safe and pleasant as well as meet the overwhelming demand for new transit systems.

Advances in technology and communication coupled with changes in the workplace and the economy could help too. I foresee a steady rise in the number of knowledge workers and a steady increase in the percentage of these workers who "telecommute" to their offices from home using computer, fax, phone and modem.

Similarly, experts believe that many shopping and personal business trips—banking, paying bills, etc.—will be obviated by the use of home-based shopping by phone, television or computer. If this is coupled with more walking opportunities for daily shopping and interaction, the result could be quite powerful. Of course, this is by no means certain, as some studies have shown that telecommuting on its own results in work trips being replaced by other trips.

But all of these options are intended to work together, providing a major shift in the convenience and accessibility of our communities. The impact would not be seen overnight, but would be gradual, over a few decades, just as the shift to suburban auto dominance has been gradual. Ultimately, however, the impact would be profound, both in reducing consumption of fossil fuels and in meeting other goals of a sustainable society, such as social equity, job creation, and enhanced quality of life.

To accomplish this "retrofitting of cities, suburbs and towns" we need a deliberate and gradual removal of government regulations and subsidies which favor decentralization and single-use auto-dependent development. In their place we would put a set of policies that encourage resource-efficient, mixed-use communities. This is not an attempt to outlaw single-family suburban development; indeed the suburb will continue to be the choice of many. But people should have a realistic, affordable choice of other kinds of communities. The market distortions, which prevent such communities from developing, should be eliminated.

Furthermore, suburban communities can be re-configured to be more efficient with mixed-use community centers and improved pedestrian and transit accessibility. After all, the work trip is a minority of all trips. Improving accessibility of shopping, schools and services can help to reduce non-work auto travel.

Along with more efficient suburban growth patterns, increasing numbers of people may prefer a more urban lifestyle. Policies should ensure that well developed livable communities are available in urban areas. This may entail both redevelopment and renovation of existing neighborhoods and new development in former industrial areas and around existing or new transit stations and downtown living. A similar opportunity exists for the redevelopment of older inner ring suburbs.

Sprawl, The Automobile and Affording the American Dream

Tremendous private and public capital is at risk of being stranded in the older shopping centers, strip malls, offices and housing subdivisions of these aging suburbs. Suburban jurisdictions and investors alike need a way to preserve the value of these investments.

This goal would be accomplished through a variety of strategies—acting in an integrated fashion with each other to provide a choice of communities and in concert with transit and other supply options to provide an alternative to solo driving. To this end, we need:

- Continued research and public education on the quality of life impacts of auto and fossil fuel dependent lifestyles. We need to document and publicize hours behind the wheel, the impacts of sedentary and obese lifestyles our children are being taught, pedestrian death tolls, the rise of road rage and aggressive driving, the increased percentage of our disposable income being expended on transportation, and the health impacts of the automobile.
- Enactment of strengthened Corporate Average Fuel Economy Standards. The CAFÉ Standard should rise to 40 miles per gallon over the next several years, and the exemption for sport utilities and light trucks must be eliminated. These vehicles could be phased in at some achievable yet tougher standard.
- A government-led public/private mixed use-financing initiative to identify and end barriers to financing of higher density, mixed-use development.
- Expansion of the program for location efficient mortgages. Fannie Mae has announced market tests of this program in Chicago, Los Angeles and Seattle.
- Extension of the regional and statewide planning structure developed under ISTEA and TEA-21 to other programs which influence and guide growth and development—HUD's new block grants, HHS service grants, etc. All should be linked to a regional structure for metropolitan planning so that housing, business development and service delivery can be regionally designed and delivered as part of regional growth strategies.

When I was growing up, getting a driver's license and access to the family car meant freedom and getting out of the house. Some part of me still carries that association, but the larger part associates driving with traffic jams, nonproductive time, and expense.

More and more, we have nowhere to go in our cars. If we surrender our towns, countryside and cities to the car, we will also be surrendering many other values that we hold dear: neighborhood life, a sense of history and place, a feeling of belonging somewhere.

Why We Need to Get Beyond the Automated Highway System

Presentation to the National Automated Highway System Assessment Committee, National Academy of Sciences, Washington, DC

October 10, 1997

Introduction
The Automated Highway Systems project has been flawed since its inception. The project has both flaws in its institutional and scientific approach and in the overall implementability of an Automated Highway System concept involving high speed platooning of vehicles in a "hands-off" mode in a real-world environment. This criticism does not imply criticism of the overall Intelligent Transportation Systems program, which has some merit through programs such as traveler information, advanced transit and traffic management, and other safety applications. Nor is the Intelligent Vehicle research being proposed to replace the AHS effort fundamentally flawed, as it focuses on providing improved safety through enhancing vehicle capabilities and ultimately the ability of the vehicle operator to respond to safety problems. Some of the research performed by the AHS Consortium may be of real benefit to this Intelligent Vehicle Initiative.

My concerns with the AHS Consortium effort are briefly summarized below.

Fatal Flaws in Design Concept, Scope and Conduct of AHS Research
- The AHS program is a solution looking for a problem. Basically the ISTEA legislation stipulated the development of an AHS prototype or demonstration, presuming that a fully automated highway was the solution to some problem. AHS promoters have ex post facto appended goals of safety, improved mobility and environmental betterment to the program, but that's beside the point. A proper research question might have been: how

can advanced telecommunication and control technologies be employed to better link the vehicle, the vehicle operator and the transportation infrastructure to optimize efficiency, safety and community and environmental benefit? Performance targets could have been set for each goal, and a fully automated highway system might have been one of the ways of reaching the goals. Presuming a technological solution before even asking the research question is bad science.

- The AHS Consortium has an inherently conflicted role. The Consortium members are charged with simultaneously developing and evaluating the Automated Highway System. As many of the consortium members stand to profit from its introduction (if public subsidy is provided for the highway infrastructure), the AHS consortium has also taken on the job of promoting the Automated Highway System through a series of expensive and heavily marketed roll-outs. To ask the same people to develop and critique a program is bad science. To have them also act to promote it is even more questionable. For the federal government to actually join the consortium as a member also raises questions about FHWA's ability to independently act to monitor the contract and assure performance and progress.
- The AHS program has lacked ongoing independent criticism, evaluation and peer review. All peer review of the program has been conducted from within the Consortium, and to the best of my knowledge, all evaluations of its environmental or societal implications have been funded by the Consortium and have remained the work product of the Consortium. This TRB review of the program is the first FHWA-funded evaluation of the program outside the control of the Consortium. There is ample precedent for ongoing peer review of these kinds of industry-government partnerships. The Partnership for a New Generation of Vehicles has benefited from an ongoing NRC panel which has issued a series of critical evaluations of the research goals, plan and methodology of the PNGV. Similarly, the Human Genome project has allocated funding for independent evaluation of the societal and ethical implications of the project.

- The AHS program lacks a true systems context. The Automated Highway System would be one new element in a complex increasingly integrated Intermodal transportation system. In addition the AHS will have complex interactions with the built and natural environment and with society as a whole. In focusing on technical feasibility and on systems engineering for the AHS system, the project has failed to conceptualize the AHS within this larger environment, and as a consequence has trivialized the real issues facing scale up on an AHS from a nifty demonstration with lots of "gee-whiz" appeal to a broadly implementable application.

Problems With Implementing an Automated Highway System
- Public Acceptability. I have seen no evidence that the public is willing to allow its daily commutes to be interrupted while an AHS is constructed within its metropolitan freeway system, or that they are willing to pay for either the public or private costs of the system. Will Americans trust government or corporations to drive their cars for them? Will they pay thousands of dollars extra to equip their automobiles to be AHS capable? Will members of the public who cannot afford to buy AHS capability accept being denied access to a portion of the highway infrastructure? Public outcry over toll proposals and HOV lanes would seem to indicate that the AHS would generate a substantial outcry over a "two-class" highway system. The AHS Consortium has devoted little attention to researching these issues.
- How can AHS be "scaled up" to a meaningful system? While we never doubted that a prototype AHS could be built (after all we've had automated train control for some time), we have long wondered where the AHS will be put in the real world. Will it take away existing freeway lanes on crowded metropolitan interstates? Will we construct second decks on top of existing freeways, or acquire entirely new rights of way? It seems unlikely that enough right of way will be found in enough places to make the AHS implementable in most metropolitan areas

across the country. If it is not available on most freeways, then how many automobile manufacturers will offer it? If few manufacturers offer it, then few people will buy AHS capability and few will use AHS lanes. The AHS Consortium has not adequately addressed this issue of scaling up from the prototype.
- The AHS will likely involve prohibitive public sector construction and operation costs. For the AHS to achieve its stated safety, mobility and environmental goals, it will have to be broadly applied in metropolitan settings all over the country. It is not clear to me where AHS lanes (typically 2-4 lanes for bi-directional flow and transition) can be placed in our already crowded metropolitan transportation systems. Either lanes will be taken out of general use or entirely new lanes will have to be constructed. The construction of new lanes will be hugely expensive and also disrupt traffic on a large scale. I have seen no evaluation of these costs, which should have been presented front and center at the San Diego roll-out.
- The claimed environmental benefits of the AHS are questionable, if not entirely spurious. AHS backers have claimed that the AHS will improve air quality by improving traffic flow. This claim appears to rest on earlier air quality models which claimed hydrocarbon benefits from increases in traffic speed. More recent models indicate that traffic flow improvements actually worsen emissions of another pollutant, NOX. In addition research indicates that most of the traffic flow improvements from added capacity are short term, as added capacity is soon filled by induced travel as motorists change routes, alter timing of their trips and make new trips. In the long run, improved throughput is not a sustainable air quality strategy.
- The AHS may have substantial negative impacts on non-automated streets and highways. If the claimed increases in capacity are real, and automated lanes actually do carry more people to downtowns and suburban activity centers, then the AHS would dump substantial additional traffic on the already overcrowded "dumb" streets of our urban and suburban business districts. The AHS backers have not modeled the system

Why We Need to Get Beyond the Automated Highway System

impacts of additional traffic carried by the AHS lanes on surface streets and other non-automated freeway lanes. The benefits could be substantially reduced.

- AHS benefits are likely to be further reduced by safety and reliability concerns. Concerns about liability (won't AHS operators be assuming liability over vehicle operations?) would be certain to lead to reductions in AHS operating speeds, to increases in following distance between platooned vehicles, to the construction of barriers to prevent vandalism and outside interference, and thus to a reduction in overall benefits as reliability, redundancy and protection from liability become more important than improved throughput and higher speeds. This tradeoff may increase AHS costs dramatically and reduce benefits at the same time.

Thinking Like a System: Operationalizing Sustainability Through Transportation Technologies

ITS World Congress, 1995 Yokohama, Japan

Today we're here to talk about the environmental impacts of Intelligent Transportation Systems, but I would like to broaden the topic to looking at the question of "sustainability." We know that sustainability is a serious concern for the gamut of interests and populations—everyone has something at stake. Take my uncle, for instance. He's a typical conservative insurance executive from Iowa and he told me recently that he's becoming worried about the viability of their industry. Their ability to predict major catastrophes based on what's happened in the past is faltering because of erratic weather patterns. To him, sustainability means not only environmental sustainability, but the ability to make a living.

Policy makers and scholars have for years attempted to define, bound, and refine the elusive concept of sustainability. The Surface Transportation Policy Projects is a coalition of groups concerned about the relationship between transportation and the economy, the environment and our social fabric. We believe that transportation policy and investment should serve the needs of people and communities, not just the needs of vehicles and facilities. For the past several months, we have been attempting to define a role for emerging transportation technology applications in creating a more sustainable global future. With the assistance of the Minnesota Department of Transportation, research team of the Humphrey Institute at the University of Minnesota, the Claremont Graduate School in Claremont, California, and the Surface Transportation Policy Project, we have tackled this task. Like many others, we are using a working definition for sustainability that includes consideration for economics, environment, and social equity issues at the community scale.

That's the easy part. The difficult task is to operationalize the concept of sustainability into an actionable agenda for the development of Intelligent Transportation Systems. STPP has been involved in a number of national initiatives on sustainability, such as the President's Council on Sustainable Development and the White House Dialogue on Greenhouse Gas Emissions from Personal Motor Vehicles. Both of these present opportunities to operationalize the concepts that we're talking about. In each, we've worked with others to develop a good set of policies to reduce vehicle miles travelled (VMT), all designed to operationalize sustainability in transportation.

When I think of sustainability, I look to systems theory as a helpful tool. Although we tend to refer to the transportation system as a system, we don't usually think of it as a system. This is one of our key problems, because transportation is indeed a large complex system that integrates people, modes and land uses. Instead, we think of single modes—we think of driving as separate from bicycling or transit, and we think of walking as something that we did when we were children. As a result, we don't know how to manage transportation as a system. Rather, we manage it as a series of incremental parts. We claim to understand the connections between all these parts, but that still doesn't seem to help us either.

We even have a hard time collecting the data. The data that we do collect shows us that the situation is not improving. VMT in the United States during the 1980s grew by 4% a year, and from 1983 to 1990 VMT increased by over 40%. Travel surveys in most metro areas from the 1990s show that we're driving more miles and spending more time driving. Also, utility is decreasing because we're making fewer trips. The increase in travel was formerly related to an increase in drivers licenses and automobiles per capita, probably a sign of economic health. Now it's more like dropping a bag of marbles, because our population and uses are spreading out, requiring us to travel farther to get the same things.

Our second key problem is greenhouse gases. Carbon dioxide emissions are increasing as we travel farther and farther every year. Today, 30% of our greenhouse gas emissions comes from motor vehicles. And consider the worldwide problems as we export inefficient technologies and management systems to the developing world. If a billion Chinese convert from bicycles to cars, we're in trouble.

A third serious issue is that there are increasing inequities in the distribution of transportation resources. One study by Michael Cameron of the Environmental Defense Fund looks at this issue. Cameron divided the population of Southern California into five income quintiles and calculated their transportation costs and benefits. He found that low-income people pay disproportionately more for the services they receive and receive fewer benefits than wealthier individuals. He then goes on to argue that pricing systems help us achieve a more equitable outcome.

Fourth, many people lack access—to jobs, health care, education, social services, shopping, and other destinations. Demographic trends seem to be exacerbating this. For example, working mothers are particularly hard hit by relying on cars, because research shows homes are located closer to where husbands work. Meanwhile, many women are saddled with child care, soccer games, and other responsibilities that make transportation a critical issue for them. Older persons also face dramatic challenges, as many age in place in the suburbs, which aren't dense enough to support transit, and where people can't get around without cars. Many rural populations are characterized by increasing isolation. And the little that we know about the travel patterns of the very poor and zero-vehicle households is also troubling. Their transportation burdens are such that after spending all their time getting to and from places, they barely have time to look for work.

We often don't understand that transportation plays a role in these social issues.

Transportation decisions are made in relation to other transportation factors, such as bottlenecks and roadway design, and not to accommodate the needs of people and communities. There are few effective ways to build external signals into our decision-making processes, no feedback loops to tell us how we're doing. Also, the segmentation in the management of the system is one of our most formidable obstacles. Currently, each owner-operator is asked to optimize travel in their respective modes, whether it's a freeway or a transit system they're trying to optimize. A land use planner tries to optimize tax revenues.

Transportation users all try to optimize their efforts too. Freight operators will ship goods long distances because they can take advantage of lower wages elsewhere.

In other words, all actors try to optimize the cheapness of the transportation system, and the result is system inefficiency and waste. Technology can help us solve some of these problems, by helping to provide feedback, giving us alternatives for dealing with problems, and showing us how our transportation can truly work as a system.

What we need is a goal framework, complete with examples of technologies that support sustainable development for communities. The main challenge is how to reconstruct the transportation system to better serve sustainable communities. Here are four ideas.

First, transportation should be conservative in nature. Natural systems are typically conservative—change slowly, evolving to changing conditions to maximize flexibility while minimizing risk. In our transportation construction era, the main priority has been the throughput of the system.

We're now at a stage where we can no longer build our way out of congestion and other problems, so throughput must be managed. Technologies can start to provide alternatives to the built options. They can also show us where we maintain what we have before we build something new. Advance public transit dispatching, scheduling and vehicle locating systems

This also involves reducing the use of non-renewable resources. Life cycle costing is part of that, as is the use of recycled materials. This is becoming a big part of the asphalt industry, and the application of technology in quality control has proven critical to this. Alternative-fueled vehicles, mobile air quality monitoring, and roadway pollution runoff monitoring also help.

Second, instead of mobility being the end all and be all of our transportation system, the main goal should be accessibility. We should look at how well we're making opportunities available to people and communities. This is where we begin incorporating social equity and social justice into our working concept of sustainability. Technology can help us measure our performance in delivering these services to people. Microsimulation and other activity-based modeling, for example, can help us reveal the number of opportunities that exist within a 20-minute walk or bike ride. We can also explore the potential of telecommuting and teleshopping to provide better access. Technology can provide us with a more comprehensive understanding of our data. For example, you could measure access to jobs for various communities, going beyond simply showing where jobs exist, to showing what kinds of skill levels are required of workers and how one could get to those jobs.

Third, transportation policy needs to be considered as strategic investment. People on both sides of the aisle are questioning the long-held assumption that transportation means jobs. Now they're asking if a given project provides more jobs than simply digging a big hole and filling it back up again. We need to target investments to make sure that they're paying off. There are two ways that investments can make a payoff. The first is illustrated by a recent German study on global climate change.

Researchers were concerned about the sustainable development impacts of the new European economic union. They started by looking at the total economic, environmental, and energy balance of creating one tin of yogurt at a local factory. They found that materials came from all over the world, and that the total social costs for creating that one tin were enormous. So part of targeting our transportation investments is considering those social costs when we develop our regional economies.

There is a need to push for a regional balance that favors the local production of goods. ITS technologies such as traffic management and traveler information that maximize system efficiency without incurring major capital and operating expenses can be considered a very good investment. The second investment rationale goes in the opposite direction. We should acknowledge that we are dealing in a global economy, and that some things need to happen to facilitate the transformation of our freight movement system into that economy. That's where intermodalism helps us the most through maximizing connections between all haulers, especially rail freight and shipping, and moving freight systems closer to regions. Providing an informed and integrated goods movement infrastructure is an essential step to ensuring the full participation of regions in this economy in an environmentally efficient manner.

Beyond showing how technology can better serve sustainable communities, there's a second set of broad goals—making the transportation system work better. That's the only way we're going to move into the future. We've already built nearly all of the highway systems in the United States that we're going to build in this century. Now our challenge is evolving from builders to managers. Part of this is employing technologies such that our transportation system meets our national goals. The traditional presumption that increased throughput is good needs to give way to the view that providing good access is the main goal and that throughput is just part of that mission. Technology should enable you to meet a balance, especially if it is put at the service of a public process that has a set of social goals. If you want to maximize throughput, it has to have a proven goal, such as diverting traffic away from historic neighborhoods.

The first internal goal is system integration. Technology can also help us better integrate and manage the transportation system, by linking freeways to transit, bikeways to local roads, etc. What we want is the ability to manage traffic dynamically in real time. Other developments, like smart cards and smart billing, could further increase intermodal connections. Smart cards will enable people to use one payment medium for all fares and smart billing means you only write one check. Rural mayday systems will eliminate some of the sense of isolation in rural communities. Navigational technologies can help everyone from out-of-town tourists to folks looking for parking.

A second key goal is to promote redundancy and flexibility in the transportation system. Systems theory tells us that the healthiest systems are the ones that are most robust, ones that can accommodate unexpected changes, ones that can adjust quickly without failing. Take the telephone system, for example. The telephone signal doesn't care if it's traveling by an NHS route, or through a little street route, or by bike or by foot. What counts is that it gets the caller there. Together, these developments mean that telecommuting, rideshare matching, and other forms of information-sharing can enhance the performance of the system.

A third key goal is incorporating the notion of feedback into the transportation system. In other words, users of the system should be aware of the applications and implications of various strategies.

This works for freight information systems, rural mayday systems, transit and traffic systems. In a way, it requires us to think forty miles upstream. I like to be able to turn on my cable TV system and see what travel conditions are going to be before I actually leave the house with a vehicle. I would like even better to be able to compare travel times under current conditions by transit with travel times by alternate auto routes. Feedback is also an important concept for traffic management and incident management.

Finally, a fourth key goal is promoting peoples' right to know. Transportation policy should be transparent, and people are entitled to understand where their investment dollars are going. Technology applications, particularly the internet, can increase the accountability of transportation institutions to the taxpaying public.

How we can operationalize all of these goals? This is a difficult task, but here are four suggestions:

1. Develop an architecture that is ends-oriented and not means-oriented. The architecture currently being developed is listed in terms of user services, but those things are virtually impenetrable to users. Instead, the architecture should be developed in terms that users understand and framed in terms of what it should deliver for users and customers.
2. We need to measure transportation system performance. We might look at carbon dioxide use per capita and accessibility indices by income, geography, and other factors using GIS software. In addition to measuring access to jobs, shopping, and other destinations, we might want to look at accessibility to markets, and link up business location to other factors. We could also look at percentages of land devoted to transportation

and try to bring that number down. Or we could look at the percentage of gross domestic product devoted to transportation. Is a bigger percentage good or bad? The answer is that it's both, and the answer depends on what you're spending your money on and what you're getting in return. There are many other things we can look at: system condition, life cycle costs, pavement condition, water quality, energy intensity, transportation costs by income, etc. But together, these performance measures could constitute benchmarks for sustainable transportation.

I'd like to close by quoting Gregory Bateson, who was a leading systems thinker, as well as a psychiatrist and an anthropologist—which is what we all need to be to work in the transportation field. He says that "the goal of our society should be a single system of environment combined with high human civilization, in which the flexibility of the civilization shall match that of the environment to create an ongoing complex system, open-ended for slow change of even basic characteristics." This could be an alternate definition of sustainability. That's where we get back to the principle of being conservative. Because our experience with the building era has shown us that we've been having fast change of basic characteristics, and we don't know what the consequences are.

Fast change is due to the introduction of technology without a value set, a needs set, or an ethics set that allow it to be applied to meet social goals. And transportation has been as much a victim of this as any other sector of our society.

About the Author

Hank Dittmar (1956–2018) is the author of *Transport and Neighbourhoods* (Edge Futures, 2008), *New Transit Town* (Island Press, 2004) and the forthcoming *DIY Cities* (Island Press, 2020). He is coauthor of *Sustainable Planet* (Beacon Press, 2000) and *Green Living* (Compendium, 2009). Before his death in 2018, he was a frequent contributor to *Building Design* magazine and also wrote for the *London Evening Standard*, *Los Angeles Times*, *The Guardian*, *The New York Times*, and *The Washington Post*.

Dittmar was the founding principal of Hank Dittmar Associates, an international urban planning firm (2013–2018). Before that, he was Chief Executive of The Prince's Foundation for Building Community for nearly a decade, and prior to that was Founding President and CEO of Reconnecting America, and Executive Director of the Surface Transportation Policy Partnership. His long and varied career included service as a regional planner, airport director, policy advisor, and outreach worker with street gangs in Chicago. He was a visiting fellow at Kellogg College at Oxford University, Outstanding Alumnus of the Graduate School at the University of Texas at Austin, and winner of the Seaside Prize for his contributions to urban design worldwide.

Island Press | Board of Directors

Pamela Murphy
(Chair)

Terry Gamble Boyer
(Vice Chair)
Author

Tony Everett
(Treasurer)
Founder,
Hamill, Thursam & Everett

Deborah Wiley
(Secretary)
Chair, Wiley Foundation, Inc.

Decker Anstrom
Board of Directors,
Discovery Communications

Melissa Shackleton Dann
Managing Director,
Endurance Consulting

Margot Ernst

Alison Greenberg

Rob Griffen
Managing Director,
Hillbrook Capital

Marsha Maytum
Principal,
Leddy Maytum Stacy Architects

David Miller
President, Island Press

Georgia Nassikas
Artist

Alison Sant
Cofounder and Partner,
Studio for Urban Projects

Ron Sims
Former Deputy Secretary,
US Department of Housing
and Urban Development

Sandra E. Taylor
CEO, Sustainable Business
International LLC

Anthony A. Williams
CEO and Executive Director,
Federal City Council

Sally Yozell
Senior Fellow and Director
of Environmental Security,
Stimson Center